Where dips the rocky highland
Of Sleuth Wood in the lake,
There lies a leafy island
Where flapping herons wake
The drowsy water rats;
There we've hid our faery vats,
Full of berrys
And of reddest stolen cherries.
Come away, O human child!
To the waters and the wild
With a faery, hand in hand,
For the world's more full of weeping than you can understand.

— William Butler Yeats, from "The Stolen Child"

Rumors *of* Water

thoughts on creativity & writing

l . l . b a r k a t

 T. S. Poetry Press • New York

T. S. Poetry Press
Ossining, New York
Tspoetry.com

Throughout this book, references are made to the following brands and sources: *Muse* magazine is a publication of Carus Publishing. Heinz is a trademark of H. J. Heinz Company. Facebook is a social networking service of Facebook, Inc. IPod is a registered trademark of Apple Inc. Christmas Tea, Bagatelle, and Polka are teas distributed by Betjeman & Barton. Twitter is a micro-blogging service of Twitter, Inc. Laity Lodge is a retreat center owned by The Foundations for Laity Renewal. TheHighCalling.org is a website sponsored by The Foundations for Laity Renewal. *I Love Lucy* is a series distributed by Paramount. Pixie Hollow and Club Penguin are virtual game worlds produced by the Walt Disney Internet Group. Pooh is a character in A. A. Milne's *Winnie the Pooh*; products now marketed by The Walt Disney Company. Land's End is a clothing retailer owned by Sears Holdings Corporation.

Cover photo by Claire Burge claireburge.com
Cover floral illustration by Sonia Joie Barkat

ISBN 978-09845531-6-7

Library of Congress Cataloging-in-Publication Data:
Barkat, L.L.
    [Memoir/Writing.]
    Rumors of Water: Thoughts on Creativity & Writing/L.L. Barkat
    ISBN 978-09845531-6-7
    Library of Congress Control Number: 2011936219

for my girls, Sara and Sonia, who make my life beautiful

Many Thanks To

Sara, who wants me to tell stories. Sonia, who is, as always, my Lovely Laughing Lady. John, who sweetly takes me back to woods and streams, even when I don't want to get off the couch. My parents, who gave me my imagination by walking me through strawberry fields or skating me across icy lakes. Mom and Dad Barkat, for your steady presence, especially in the lives of our girls. My online community, that graciously both gives me words and receives mine in return. Some of you even helped me develop this book one Saturday morning, by adding your voice to the Twitter stream when I asked, *What should I write?* You may see yourselves here, and I hope it will make you smile. Sam Van Eman, only a brave man agrees to edit someone as strong-minded as me. You get the prize for courage and gentility; I owe you a cup of Bagatelle tea. Laura Boggess, for reading the manuscript and loving it; we all need people who delight in our words. Bradley J. Moore, also for reading, and for offering kind words and excellent feedback. And for the team at *The High Calling.org* and everyone who encourages with blog comments and retweets, cards and tea cozies, aprons or pottery, know that your love gives me a reason to keep writing.

Table of Contents

MOMENTUM

1 Rumors

How it Begins

I am trying to have a conversation about writing. About how I can't write anymore. Or at least how I can't seem to write anything sustained. My older daughter Sara is trying to listen in, as is her way these days.

"Can you find me some water?" I ask. I've been sitting at this picnic for hours and really could use a cup of something simple to drink. I could also use a few minutes alone with my friend Anne, to work out this question of writing and creativity and what seems to be standing in my way.

Before I can form another thought, Sara is back. "There are rumors of water," she says. "But I couldn't find any."

"Rumors of water," I answer. "Now that's a good book title."

"It could be about you and your daughters," says Anne. "How you're raising them to be so creative."

I turn this thought around in my mind. "I don't feel like I've finished living that enough," I say, knowing this is both true and not true at all.

I have been trying to write while raising my girls. I have been struggling. There are days I feel wildly creative; there are weeks when I feel ground down and completely spent. I am trying to show my girls that creativity is theirs for the taking. Sometimes it seems to be. Sometimes I feel the road is so long they will never get where they're trying to go.

There are so many things standing in my way this morning, I can hardly begin. Yet I've heard there are rumors of water. Maybe that is enough.

2 How Will We Eat?

Let the Writing Be

Today my younger daughter Sonia is in need of direction, and despite wanting to be alone with my thoughts and my writing, I remind myself: I signed on for this when we decided to home educate our girls. I signed on for the questions, the need for suggestions, the challenges to my own creativity that have just now made me think to put my daughter on the porch with Julia Kasdorf.

Sonia's cursive book is nowhere to be found. Where do these things go when I'm not looking? It could make me crazy if I let it. Maybe that's why, in the absence of the cursive book, I give her a pencil, a notebook, and Kasdorf's poem, "When Our Women Go Crazy."

"Copy this in cursive," I say.

"I can't do Z's," she says back.

My heart-rate quickens, and I blink hard. *I signed on for this. I signed on for this.* I take her pencil and write the whole alphabet in cursive.

"Your F and your B look the same," she observes.

When our women go crazy, says Julia's poem, they keep asking… *how will we eat? Who will cook? Will there be enough?* The refrigerators of these crazy women are always *immaculate and full,* just as when these women are sane.

Who are these women? I am not like them. Sane or crazy, my refrigerator is always doing science experiments that involve organic vegetables trying to go back to their roots. Some of these vegetables even sprout roots before they become primordial soup fit for the compost pile.

I am not like these women. Or maybe I am. *How will I write? Who will cook up fresh ideas? Will there be enough?* I try to stack the day in my direction, make it immaculate and full.

"Do you like my poem?" Sonia comes in the back door and presses her notebook into my hands. "I'm hungry," she says, then frowns about the frying pan being dirty, because she wants to make an egg. I do not remind her that the pan is dirty because she made an egg yesterday and neglected to clean up.

In the hands of my younger daughter, Julia's poem has taken on a new shape. Most of the original line breaks are gone. Now the poem breaks where the page ends and it takes up a lot more space. Plurals have become singular. There are crossouts and inverted add-this-here carats where words were forgotten then later added. *Sane* has become something like *rain,* spelled *sain.*

Every piece of writing tries to go back to its roots. I should know this by now—so many essays under the bridge; three books, each of which I eventually fought the same identity battle with. A piece of writing knows what it wants and needs to be, but we get in the way. We want something serious to be funny, because we notice that funny writers are popular. We can write funny, we want to be popular, so we try to foist humor upon the work. It refuses. We want to be urbane; our writing wants to live in the country. We want a three-hundred page treatise; our words want to be a brief offering on the subject. We want to write sophistication; the work reminds us, "You are currently living a life of dirty frying pans and letter F's that look like B's."

Sonia reshaped the Kasdorf poem without thinking. Her essential self bubbled to the top. I don't think she struggled with this.

So now I am musing. I should spell *sane* like *sain* too—let the unrestrained rain of *my own life* infuse my writing. Let the *me-I-am-right-now* simply be.

3 Purple Moths

Don't Be Idealistic

The basement is dark and musty. This is no surprise, as basements go. I transfer white clothes from the dryer to a broken plastic laundry basket, extricate the brights from the washing machine, dump too many darks into the freed-up space and notice that the garbage needs to be taken out.

How will I write?

I know how books are supposed to be structured. When I publish other authors I'm careful to help them know what books should look like. Readers like a *do-able* book of about twelve to fifteen chapters. The chapters should all run about the same length. Readers like symmetry.

Today the piano teacher canceled our lesson. She is sick. Tomorrow, at our home education co-op, we will need to substitute for a child who was supposed to be presenting about Outer Space. This weekend I had plans to write, but my younger daughter promised to help out at a Benefit Picnic. I made a super-spicy chili bean salad and it all got eaten.

Sometimes life has no symmetry.

I drag the slate blue garbage bin out to the curb. This bin was not my idea. It is too big for me to handle. I try to forget that. It's just garbage, after all. My eye catches sight of something blue in the driveway. A small shell, only half. Must have been a robin's egg. There is no bird, so I can't prove this was a hatching. I pick up the shell and bring it into the house to show the girls.

"It's a beautiful shell," says Sonia. "So tiny," says my older daughter Sara.

"Want to hear my story?" says Sonia cheerfully. She is already moving on to her own agenda.

"Sure," I say.

The story is about a girl who is drawing a purple moth as large as a dragon. The moth has teeth and is holding something like spears. The girl is not paying attention in class, so she misses the lesson about the Space Race. But she has a purple moth to show for it.

Maybe the reason I have not been able to write in any sustained way is just this: I've been too stuck on what ought to be. I know what books look like, and the one I can write just now is more like a purple moth, half of a blue shell in the driveway, an afternoon needing to be rescheduled.

I consider my options. I can forget about writing another book. Nobody is going to fault me for not writing. Or I can make a chili bean salad of sorts, for a weekend that isn't going my way.

All of my favorite writing books have their quirks. Why can't mine have its quirks too? I suddenly remember Natalie Goldberg's *Writing Down the Bones*. It is structurally asymmetrical. The chapters are all different sizes. There are bunches of them, some as short as one or two pages. Some focus on philosophy, some on practice. If there is any symmetry at all, it is the symmetry of Natalie. She is in every chapter.

I ponder Natalie's success. *To heck with structural symmetry,* I think. I am going to write this book. There will be a purple moth in every chapter. I am not sure whether it will have teeth, especially on cranky days. But it might drink ice water, infused with mint and rose petals from the garden.

4 Plastic Flutes

Be Idealistic

Sometimes we get stuck in the basement. Nothing is surprising. What's worse, there are three loads of laundry we have to sort into predictable piles: whites, brights, darks. We twist the dials in the same direction, add the liquid soap as usual.

My basement has the annoying quality of being home to food moths. It is my own fault for leaving grains in plastic bags, oats in paper. The only thing that cheers me about this situation is how I find myself thinking of Anne Overstreet's poem, "This Has Been a Summer of Moths."

Did Anne leave grains unattended in paper bags too? I don't know, but she turned the experience into a poem I carry with me...

As if born the moment
we opened to the dark,
as if they'd been breeding
behind thyme, the tin of Earl Grey...

Standing over the washing machine, looking in, I think of Anne's poem. It would take too much to write a poem about the collars I've just scrubbed with stain remover. *There is nothing here for me.* Shirts, a few stray socks, a pair of shorts not-like-the-others that I am putting in with this load anyway, hoping the stain remover will not bleach the shorts fabric into an accidental floral pattern.

I turn on the delicate cycle, and water begins filling the machine. I open the laundry detergent. *There is nothing here for me.* Suddenly, I hesitate with the liquid soap. Bring it to my mouth and blow across it. A bubble forms, floats down to the shirts and pops. I dump the soap too soon, miss my chance for trying to make another bubble. The clear cap is empty now. I begin to screw it back on the detergent, but wait. Maybe I can make a sound with it.

I blow over the top. Nothing. This laundry-soap cap makes a terrible flute.

A vision of my mother-in-law flits through my mind. Last night my fourteen-year-old daughter Sara decided that Grandma needs to learn an instrument. My girl wished it could be piano, "but I can't bring the piano to her," she lamented. Thus, the brown plastic recorder with an ivory tip.

My mother-in-law is suffering from worn-out knees. She had one replaced last year, and she just had orthoscopic surgery on the other. Her days look much the same. Sit on the couch. Take a pain-killer. Fall asleep. My daughter sees an opportunity. If Grandma is going to sit here in the darkness of loneliness and injury, then she has time to practice on a plastic flute.

Drawing out two recorders, Sara faces her grandmother. "This is how you hold it, Grandma," she says, guiding old fingers, that are without their usual red nail polish, onto small holes. "Put it in your mouth, Grandma. No, put it in more. You're letting it slide to the edge. Put it like this, Grandma." She moves the mouthpiece to the center of tired lips.

"How do I make a song?" asks her grandmother.

"First you have to make the sounds, Grandma. We'll work on that first."

The sounds Grandma makes are all the same. It is hard to cover the holes completely, to make a new sound. Sara explains how air-flow works—that air will take the shortest route out of the instrument. "If you don't cover the holes all the way, the air will come out here." She points to the hole directly beneath the mouthpiece. This has become science lesson as much as music lesson, and Grandma is focused intently on Sara's face, ignoring knee pain for longer than she has in weeks.

When it is time to go, my mother-in-law wants to keep the recorder. "Can we put it somewhere safe?" she asks.

I glance to Sara. We both know that the recorder could be lost by the time we come back. Sara looks at me and raises her eyebrows as a silent question.

I whisper aside, "We can get a new one if she loses it."
We leave the recorder on the bookshelf.

5 Teapot Trees & Strawberries

On Inspiration

Unless we have knee problems, it is not outside the realm of possibility to go for an outing. It is Friday and I put my writing aside in exchange for Linsay's farm. I am tired anyway. Words are coming slow.

My girls went to Linsay's farm yesterday as a special trip with their enrichment class. "You have to go," they told me, clinging to handfuls of flowers they'd picked on the property— magenta and white peonies (one with the ants still on it), wild pink roses, green penny weed (I don't know the proper name for it, but it looks like tiny translucent coins), purple asters, wild yellow irises, daisies, clovers, and something that the land offers as a kind of baby's breath.

"You have to taste the strawberries!" they chimed.

"Sparkle!" said my younger daughter Sonia, who has a mind for names and details.

"Heirloom," said Sara, who cares about preserving the past, keeping memories and the beauty that came before us.

It is a mistake for a writer to pass up this kind of passion: two girls clutching peonies, with the taste of the reddest strawberries they ever saw still on their tongues. Writing starts with living. Living starts with somebody caring so much about something that they need to drag you out of your writing chair and take you where you'll be surprised to find your words.

I find more words at Linsay's place than I've discovered in a long time. I find a teapot tree with cobalt, crimson, and copper kettles hanging from it. Some of the pots hold dirt and star-leaved nasturtiums. Near the makeshift tree (actually an enormous branch that Linsay rescued after a storm and put into the ground), is a greyed picnic table, with a crystal pitcher of mint and lemon ice water. Next to it, small-handled drinking glasses are upside down, waiting for someone in need of refreshment. A jar of raw honey invites dipping. I do, though I'm not sure where to put the spoon after, and I wish I could lick it.

There is a stuga (not a cottage, say my girls— a *stuga*, because that's what Linsay called it yesterday, and it is where Linsay and her siblings used to sleep on summer nights when they were children).

The stuga holds more words: Jemima's oversized duck eggs in a cooler (and all I can picture is Beatrix Potter's lady duck with her blue bonnet); worn wooden planks; porcelain; kale; greens with pink rose petals, purple clover and marigolds; sugar snap peas I forget to buy because thoughts of Jemima distract me; creamy lavender soaps, handmade; a tiny counter piled with speckled notebooks where Linsay records her transactions.

There are so many words I can't collect them all—a midnight black steed the girls say a knight should ride; Sweetie tomatoes; parsley, sage, rosemary and red-hot chili peppers; aubergines and garden air that makes me want to breathe it forever.

6 Japanese Beans

Write with What You Have

Aduki Bean Salad comes in three spellings, at least that is what Sara discovered when she went searching for a recipe. Adzuki. Azuki. Aduki. No matter how you spell it, the salad uses pert brown beans, compact and full of protein.

I was not thinking about the protein when I asked her to look for a recipe. I was thinking about all the dried beans I've accumulated over the past few years. Many of them are sitting in the basement in bulk plastic bags. Some of them (legumes like green lentils, or red) were ruined by the food moths.

Lately I have felt overwhelmed by the beans in my life, or, more accurately, the beans in my basement. So I vowed to stay away from the health-food store for as long as I could, or at least until I got bored of trying to make a life with beans.

Enter the Aduki Bean Salad.

It is the last day of my girls' educational enrichment program, where they go once a week, and where, among other things, they ride a seesaw to power a chicken-house and occasionally cook for a local soup kitchen. On the last day, the program always holds a little graduation ceremony where the teachers say wonderful things about each child, like, "This certificate is awarded to Sara for her indefatigable love of Sherlock Holmes," or, "This certificate is awarded to Sonia for her tenacious pursuit of committing to memory the entire history of *I Love Lucy*."

I am sure the teachers will say other things this year, about my girls being good at art or being faithful friends. But they could just as well discuss Sherlock Holmes and Lucy, both of whom I wish would come and entertain my bean-laden basement.

After the ceremony, there is always a potluck lunch. Committed to taking advantage of my bean storehouse, I decide to make Aduki Bean Salad.

Aduki beans are versatile. Used in everything from ice cream and tea to dumplings and biscuits, they can go sweet or nutty, move seamlessly between dinner and dessert. They're a cultivated vining bean, not found in the wild; somebody has to take care to bring them into the world.

I like that the name for Aduki beans, in Japanese, means *small bean*. I like that they are used in ceremonial dishes or just in potluck salads. I like that they are high in iron and are valued for their healing properties.

The recipe that Sara found for Aduki Bean Salad called for shallots, tomatoes, and parsley. That sounded very nice, for a house in possession of those things. But my house is offering dandelion greens, chives, mint, and oranges.

As a writer, I have learned that when a job needs to get done, there is little use fussing about the lack of necessary ingredients like tomatoes and parsley. I have learned that if I can't go to Japan, I can go to a bean that tirelessly embodies a certain history in Asian cuisine. I've learned that oranges and mint are a fine substitution for apple cider vinegar and black pepper.

This is the secret of the prolific writer. To agree to use small beans and the ingredients at hand. To cultivate out of potlucks and basement-bargains.

If we have been working on the same novel for ten years, or are still writing the history of the Aduki bean after researching it for a lifetime, that is okay. In the writer's life, there are no rules about timing or quantity. Still, it might be worth asking ourselves if we have at our fingertips some small beans, just waiting for cultivation or chives.

7 August Beautiful

Be Flexible

"Did you practice your recorder, Grandma?" my older daughter Sara asks.

"I don't know where it is."

Sara looks on the shelf. The recorder is safe and unplayed after a week of sitting. My younger daughter Sonia picks it up and starts playing loudly. Grandma smiles, leans on her cane, then limps into the family room and sits on the couch.

"Let's play a word game," Sara suggests. She has followed her grandmother and is now sitting on the floor at her feet. Grandpa comes in from the garage. "Let's play a word game," Sara tilts her head and addresses him. "It's an alphabet game. You take turns saying words in order of the alphabet. You have to remember all the words that other people say before you and then say them before you say your next word."

Grandpa sits down on the bed that has been in the family room since Grandma got her knee surgery and can't climb stairs. "Okay," he nods. He knows this game.

"I'll start," says Sara. "August."

"August. Beautiful," he adds.

"Your turn, Grandma."

"Very hot."

"No, Grandma," Sara laughs. "It has to be one word that starts with a C! And you have to repeat everybody else's words."

"August. Beautiful. Very hot," Grandma repeats.

Sara coaches her again. "No, you need a C-word!"

"August. Beautiful. Church," says Grandma.

When the alphabet comes around to F, we say, "Grandma, give us an F-word." We laugh again. (Not THE F-word, just AN F-word, we warn).

Grandma seems stumped, so Grandpa counsels her in their mother tongue. Sara protests, "You can't tell her what to say!

No, she can't say *food* now!"

Grandma thinks hard. "Fat," she says, without repeating everyone else's words.

We make exception, and move on.

This is what good writers often do too: move on. Maybe the plan to write a memoir isn't working out. We have given it our best shot, but for all intents and purposes, it is sitting on the shelf and we can't get it to play the song we'd envisioned. We can keep writing the memoir. That's an option. Or we can move on to another game.

My older daughter has, as she puts it, "a zillion works in progress." They are not really works in progress. They are pieces she started and never found a way to finish. They are evidence of resilience. She has not stopped writing. She has just stopped writing a zillion pieces that didn't work out.

Sometimes people ask me about this. About whether it bothers me that she doesn't finish the writing. Some of these people have been encouraging their kids to finish pieces, occasionally to the point of making the children cry and declare a hatred for writing.

It doesn't bother me that my daughter has unfinished work. I think about the larger work it all represents. In one piece I can see she's been playing with setting. In another, she has paid close attention to dialog. One exhibits good pacing. Another has a terrific narrative voice. Someday it will all come around. She'll put everything together, in a different work that no one could predict, and all the practice she did along the way will make for a wonderful piece.

"Naughty," says Grandma, when the game comes to the letter N. She has forgotten everyone else's words and has not said them. She is smiling at Sara, looking her straight in the eye.

8 Bishops & Gophers

Expect Challenges

"There are potatoes in both of your beds," I say.

My girls are puzzled by the proclamation, look at each other, then at me. Suddenly, they both start laughing, realizing I'm talking about their newly-bestowed garden beds, which I had finally given up on and then planted a bunch of potatoes in (because I found the potatoes in the basement, long-rooted and looking like aliens).

Sara is weeding. Sonia is supervising. I am obviously the accidental entertainment.

It is hot, and Sara has tied back her long dark hair. She leans towards her garden bed and asks, "What's this weed?"

"That's Bishop's Weed."

"I hate it," she says. Bishop's Weed is hard to successfully remove. It has invaded our yard, and now this bed. Sara has only been a gardener for ten minutes, and she already hates the weed.

"It's your nemesis," I say. "Every gardener has a nemesis."

Sara laughs. Fourteen years old, and she already has a nemesis. It's not as sinister as Darth Vader. It's not going to cause psychological distress and end up in her memoirs. But it's not going to go away either. She's going to need to work around it, dig it out, ignore it, accept it, if she wants to grow lettuce and peas in this garden bed.

"You should read *Second Nature*," I tell her. "It's by that guy Michael Pollan. Remember, you read an excerpt of his book *The Omnivore's Dilemma* in your *Muse* magazine?"

She remembers.

"You should read this other book by him, this gardening book," I tell her. "It's older, but it's very funny. He has a nemesis—it's a gopher, or something like that. I don't want to ruin the story of his battle with the gopher, but it involves gasoline and a match. Kind of disrupts his garden a little."

Sara's eyes open wide, then she turns back to digging out the Bishop's Weed.

I suspect that every writer has a nemesis too. Some people will say it's The Censor—a prohibitive voice that's a combination of all the naysayers we ever met or lived with in our lives. Some people will say it's The Market, always demanding writing that's saleable, preventing us from success with our memoirs that include childhood gophers and potatoes in our beds. Some people will say it's The Procrastinator, keeping us from writing about the gophers.

I am not going to tell anyone who her nemesis is. Some of us may be in need of a censor (occasionally called an "Editor"). Some of us may be writing exactly what the market wants and ignoring what we want (to our personal creative detriment). We may be up at all hours, losing sleep, working too hard at our writing, because we haven't learned to trust that it will still be there if we take a break and even procrastinate a little.

Though I won't try to pinpoint anyone's nemesis, I can suggest that working through a book like *The Artist's Way* might free us up, give insight, keep us from resorting to gasoline and matches as we face the things that hinder our best writing. I can say that it helps to read about other writers' processes and maybe see ourselves more clearly, as we identify (or not) with what these writers reveal. I can say that we should pay attention to our frustrations and our joys with writing; they might have something important to tell us. I can say that just when we figure out what our nemesis is and how to work around it, the game will change.

Sara finishes her weeding. For now, the bed seems free of Bishop's Weed. She makes little trenches and drops in far too many lettuce seeds. I can see she's a bit like me when it comes to gardening— ignoring some of the details that will assure a good harvest. But she's happy, and that's worth a lot.

I go in the house and order *Second Nature* from the library. It will be a nice diversion to read about someone else's nemesis.

VOICE

9 Do You Talk?

Listen to Your Own Voice

"It's going to be about a girl who's twelve like me. It's going to be one of those calm stories that happens."

Sonia is on her belly, on top of my white comforter, tangerine plastic notebook open in front of her. From here, she can see the river if she looks up, though right now she is busy telling me about the story she wants to write.

"What should her last name be? Her first name is Joy."

My girls are always asking me about character names, as if I could supply the perfect choices that are somehow eluding them. I always say the same thing. "Why don't you write about the character a little first, and the name will probably reveal itself." They always say the same thing in return, "I can't write the story without the names! The names tell me what they're going to be like, what they'll do."

I am looking out the window, noticing the mountains over the river. I am thinking that I just lost my chance to read *The Art of the Sonnet*. I am listening to my girl's voice, which sounds to me like what I imagine the rainbow in a fresh-blown bubble would sound like if it could speak.

"This story is going to be written in the first person. I thought of a wonderful ending for it too. The last line. This book is going to be called *Just Joy*."

My girl is wearing blue shorts that remind me of the water near St. John's island. She is wearing a loose ivory shirt that still belongs to her sister. Her feet are swinging up, down, up, down— thumping against her bottom, then thumping against her father's pillow.

"The inside flap says…" she chatters on, already having composed the marketing copy for a book that doesn't have a first page.

"At the end, Joy finds out that the meaning of life for her is just to enjoy it," she says. Then she summarizes this idea tidily in another sentence, which I forget immediately, because I am watching her wiggle, and I am watching how she grips her pencil in an unconventional way when she gets excited.

"What was it?" she looks over to me and asks.

"What was what?"

"The last line."

"Try to remember, and write it yourself," I say. "So it'll be in your voice."

Writers worry a lot about this, about voice. They are always wondering if they have one, and if not, how they can find one. The truth is that every writer has a voice. It is probably best heard by listening to oneself speak. However, once a writer starts setting down words, a process of elimination and substitution begins. A writer thinks there is a *way to sound* on the page, and reaches for it. Sometimes this works out okay; often, it makes for stilted language or turns the writer into an accidental copycat.

In my work as an online Managing Editor, I sometimes say things like this to the editors I work with: "Watch out for the Ann Voskamp stage; almost everyone who reads Ann's blog ends up dropping articles. Put the *the*'s and the *an*'s back in. Cultivate the writer's own voice. If the writer is resilient, you can even mention what you noticed about them mimicking Ann's voice, and note what you're doing to help change the situation."

Now I am listening again to my daughter's voice, as she thinks through what she wants to compose. "Because I am just Joy, and that's the way I like it," she says. "I think that'll be a good book if I ever write it."

I like the way she sounds as she keeps thinking out loud. Ironically, I notice that for the first time ever her out-loud voice conflicts with the part she actually wrote down and read to me somewhere around the moment I was thinking about St. John's island. The words she read sounded like someone else's voice. I want to say, "Tell it in your kind of words. Tell it like the purple moth story."

10 Ignoring Grandma

The Voice of Others

"You should call your grandma," I say. "She likes to hear your voice. It cheers her up. You know, she's in that house all the time, doesn't get to see people much."

Sara is writing and doesn't particularly want to be interrupted, but she goes off and does what I've asked. I hear her tell her grandmother about the new garden bed, and how she hopes to harvest lettuce from it once the seeds grow. They talk beans and basil, beets and sugar snap peas. They talk about grandma's nemesis, the groundhog, and how he steals her strawberries. They talk about stories that Sara is writing. They talk for a long, long time.

"She is the best," says Sara, after hanging up the phone. "Sometimes I don't even hear what she says."

"What?" I ask.

"I get lost in the sound of her voice. I just like to listen to it, it's so beautiful. Then I don't hear what she's saying."

My girls are good at listening to the voices of other people. They take in the sounds, the rhythms. My younger daughter Sonia can even reproduce these sounds with surprising accuracy. Sometimes she takes me South, or to London, or to Italy, with her imitative voice. Or she takes me to palaces, picnics, or the living room of *I Love Lucy*.

While it is true that writers have distinctive voices, our voices are not entirely unique. The voices of others fill our minds. Voices from the porch outside our childhood home, voices from *I Love Lucy*, voices over the phone or the iPod®. We've heard French and it has sneaked into the way we say, "My dear." We've heard street talk, and it has sneaked into the way we say, "You rock, dude." We've tucked away the voice of our grandmother, and it shows up somewhere, gentle, on the page.

This is not a bad thing. It's a human thing. It means we are in tune with the sounds others make. It might even mean we are showing love by taking these sounds into our bodies and making them our own by folding them into our writing.

I look to my own Sara, note the way her dark eyes seem happy after talking with her grandmother. "So you listen but you don't hear?" I say, laughing.

"Um, hm," she says, and laughs, sounding a bit like me.

11 French & Spanish Tea

The Voice of Passions

I am opening a jar of green tea from Granada, Spain. The jar is an old salsa jar, without its label. The tea is silvery and reminds me of those pictures I've seen of the mountain mist in China. There are curls of lavender flowers. Bits of orange peel. I am not surprised about the peels. When we went to Granada, we were told that a nearby city, Sevilla, blooms with orange-scented flowers so strong you can almost smell them in your dreams. When the flowers fall, the oranges come. On every tree-lined street, there is citrus for the taking.

This morning, I am making Te Granada, sharing it with Sara. This is the kind of sharing I feel I could do forever.

"We should do a tea pilgrimage," I say.

"What's that?"

"I don't know," I say. "Maybe we read everything we can find about tea. Maybe we try new teas from around the world. You could keep a journal. We could write poems. We could go to Kathleen's Tea House, for scones and Crème Earl Grey."

She agrees, and finds a pink journal with green flowers. She makes a declaration page, for those who want to say *yes* to the journey. She makes lines for signatures. I sign mine, "Mommy."

I open the computer, go to our local library's site, and type in *tea*. A book comes up: *Tea With Jane Austen,* and I order it. Over the next month, after dinner with my girls, I share the words of this book. We read of tea in England, of how Jane would have made toast with an iron contraption, and how she held the key to the tea cabinet. Tea was so expensive in Jane's time that servants would steal it to resell. A servant not inclined to steal might save the used leaves and peddle them. Charlatans made tea from poisonous tree leaves, added coloring and sometimes dung, and put it up for sale. The British became so enamored with tea that they went

into national debt over it. The plan for extrication from this
dilemma? Sell opium to their tea trader: China.

The girls and I try new teas. We place our orders with daddy-
the-world-traveler. He brings home Christmas Tea and Bagatelle,
from Betjeman and Barton, located in Paris. I become so enamored
with these teas that I trade in my standing order for chocolate and
make it tea. The girls steal away with cups of Christmas Tea,
regardless of the season. I discover that Betjeman and Barton do
not distribute through channels in the U.S., so my new habit will,
of necessity, take me to their online French catalog, where every
tea sounds like heaven, with roses and sunflowers or orange peels
and cherries.

To have a voice, a writer must have passions and a sense of
place. These passions and their places infuse the writing with
silvery leaves and orange peels, versus, say, ocotillo and pequins.
The words of a region, a philosophy, a passion for French or
French tea, come with their own sounds and rhythms and
fragrances. If we read the Palestinian poet Darwish, for instance,
we will find ourselves mouthing, *jasmine, doves, olives, veils.* Whereas
if we read a poet like Marcus Goodyear, we will find ourselves
breathing to the staccato of *cactus, cattle, tree poker.*

Sometimes aspiring writers ask me if they should get a
degree in writing, or go to a lot of writer's conferences. A writing
degree and a conference will help us make valuable professional
connections. They might inspire (or require) us to write. Which is a
good thing. But we don't need either of these experiences to find
and use our voice. Our voice will be better developed if we spend
time with our passions. Learn the difference between a tangerine
and a tangelo. Consider the variation in their blooms, and the place
where their nectar beads.

I pour a tea called Polka into two cups, one for Sara, one for
me. It is dotted with sunflower petals. If this tea could smile and
speak, it would tell us of its home, first in the mountains of China
or India, then somewhere in the sun-kissed countryside of France.

12 First Fireflies

Nurturing Voice through Tenderness

"Do you think it's the season for fireflies?" Sonia asks.

We have just pulled in the driveway, and night-dew has descended. I open my door to get out. "Maybe," I say.

"I haven't seen any yet," she sighs.

Sonia loves fireflies. She can catch as many as five or six at a time, somehow luring them to her soft skin and giving them a warm place to settle. On night walks, Sonia becomes our natural lantern, speaking tenderly to the fireflies, carrying them for a while.

Now we are walking up the steps, and she notices one. The first of the season. "I see one!" she shouts and runs to the grass. The glow is near the pink rosebush I bought her a few years back. It was her birthday, and that's all she wanted. A rose.

Tonight, satisfied that Sonia will soon be tender-whispering to her catch, I continue on to the house. Turn the key. Enter the hall, smiling. I am lost in thoughts of Sonia and her fireflies. I am remembering years past, our walks, and how much I love this girl.

"Mommy!" a shriek pierces.

Sonia is pushing through the door. "Mommy, a spider. Mommy," she is trembling all over, pulling my arm. "You have to save it, Mommy. A spider's web. The spider. How could he? Don't let it eat the firefly!" We are in a moment of timeless dance. She is shaking, crying, pulling, pushing. I rush out the door, and she follows.

"Near the roses! Right there, Mommy. Is it? Is it still alive?"

Writing can be a tender process, as we open ourselves to our deepest loves and dreams, as we stir up memories and carry them along. Our thoughts, like fireflies, tease and beckon. We tease and beckon too, enamored with the possibility of touching the magical transience of words and sharing them with the world.

If we are writing from deep places, fear can all but overtake us sometimes. If we are speaking with a true voice, anxiety can stop us in our tracks. Maybe we grew up in a context where no one really listened to us, or we were often told to be quiet. Maybe a teacher criticized us for writing in incomplete sentences or with a voice that seemed too wild. Perhaps we are afraid of the rawness of what we have to say, and how we want to say it. We need to find people who will provide a safe writing space for us, where criticism comes late and love and delight come early.

My girls have been writing since they were very little. "You just wrote for two hours," I would say to them, after they'd been doing what they call *playing story*. This puzzled them at first. Most kids they knew were writing according to assignments, struggling to put things they didn't care about on paper.

"We didn't do any writing," my girls would say.

"Yes you did," I'd say back. "*Playing story* is composing. Composing with words is writing, whether or not you put it on paper."

This went on for years. Then one day their handwriting caught up to their imaginations, and they started putting things on paper. I never assigned them anything. They were so full of their own ideas. When they shared their poems and stories with me, I looked for the good stuff. "I like this part," I'd say, ignoring the parts that didn't work. There were days I wondered if I was betraying The Sacred Circle of the Red Pen. But I felt strongly that what my girls needed at this tender stage was feedback about what was working. "Do more of this," I'd say. "I really like the sound, the images in this part."

Tonight, the image of the firefly in the web is horrifying. Such a small thing, really. Just another insect that flew too close to a hungry spider. But to my girl it is a tragedy-in-process. I pick up a twig and pry the firefly loose from the web. It is glowing softly, like a quiet wish.

"Can you save him?" Sonia's voice trembles.

I hold it towards the streetlamp, and can see that the firefly is already tightly woven. The spider has done its work quickly. It's possible that he has even already enjoyed some of the firefly's body, as an evening snack.

"It's okay, Honey," I say.

I turn my back to my girl and lay the firefly in night-wet grass.

"I'm going to put him here, Sweetie."

"Will the spider eat him?"

"No, no, Honey. I'll put him over here."

I shift the twig a little, act like I am making everything okay. The body of the firefly is still glowing when I wrap my arm around my girl, walk her back to the house, and shut the door.

13 Sister Love

Nurturing Voice through Critique

Sonia had read it to me first. I listened, enjoyed the sound of her voice, watched her legs swinging and her brown hair falling past her face.

Then she went off to share it with her sister...

> *Joy is entering 7th grade, but this year things are different. Because she has noticed that everyone else in her grade has something about them that's special. There is Katrina the Math Whiz and Joe the Soccer Star. But nobody calls her anything like that. Just Joy. And she wants to find what she's magnificent at. So she journeys through her twelfth year being normal and nothing for anyone to talk about. Trying to discover what she is good at, yes. But even more than that, what the meaning of life is for her.*

"I think I hurt her feelings," Sara says to me now. We are sitting at the table in our sunset yellow dining room, eating leftover rice and spicy lentils.

"What do you mean?" I ask.

"Sonia read her *Just Joy* story to me, and she asked if I liked it, and I said, 'No.'"

"Hmmm," I say.

"The thing is, she didn't give me a chance to think about it. She just asked, and I said I didn't like it. I guess...I guess I shouldn't have said that."

"Why did you?"

"I don't know. I think, it made me feel... it made me feel *sideways*."

As writers, we sometimes put aside our true voice in exchange for another. We have our reasons, sometimes invisible to us. And the result can be less than enchanting. Or sometimes we mix voices in one piece, and the reader balks. This happened to me when I was working on my first memoir. The Reader feedback came, and it was unforgiving, even angry. One editor suggested I get rid of all the opening vignettes entirely. I cried for two days. The poetic vignettes, I knew instinctively, were the life-blood of the work. If I cut them, I would kill something vital. Still, I finally began to question, "Where's the truth in this? How can I respond?"

I took the feedback to my sister, who gave me wise advice. "You're just mixing two voices," she said. "Bring the poetic voice down a notch. Bring the humorous voice down a notch too. Then they won't compete with each other so much."

It took a lot of work to incorporate my sister's advice, but I did. In the end, it saved the vignettes. Most people who read that book thank me for the vignettes and say these are their favorite parts. I want to say, "Thank my sister."

Now, eating lunch with my Sonia's big sister, I say, "It's okay that you didn't like it. I know what you mean. I felt the same way. It didn't have the energy of Sonia's voice."

"I think she must have gotten that voice from reading *Clarice Bean,*" says Sara. "But I still think I shouldn't have said 'No' like that."

"Maybe not," I say. "But she needs to hear the truth. Sometimes it's just a matter of timing, or how we say it. Sometimes we need to say something good first. Like in this case, what she read to you was a good book-jacket summary. You could acknowledge that kind of thing before you give her the critique."

"Yeah," says Sara.

Then we say how much we like the rice and spicy lentils, and how they seem to have gotten spicier overnight. We agree that Sonia, our little spicy girl, would like them too.

HABITS

14 Dishes on the Red Sled

Do You Play?

I have a clog in my drain. It stops kitchen-life as I know it. But I am so overwhelmed by my current schedule, and Wednesday's flat tire, and an article due on Friday, that I don't bother to call the plumber.

My girls peek outside and discover that I've set up kitchen-shop by the hose. I am dipping dishes in a silver bowl of water and suds, then rinsing them with a barely-controlled spray that is speckling my glasses and my tan leather sandals.

"Can I do the dishes, Mommy?" asks Sonia. This is an unusual request, coming from my eleven-year-old.

"Okay," I say.

Before I know it, Sonia has been joined by Sara, and they have upgraded the dish-doing station. A red sled serves as a drain-board. One silver bowl is for sudsy water. Another has been added, for rinsing. Somebody starts composing a song about spaghetti.

I have a psychologist friend who has told me that when children start singing, it signals that they're cognitively engaged, even cognitively growing at that very moment. This thing about singing: it was one of the reasons I first floated the idea of home educating our girls.

I'd already planned to register Sara for kindergarten, but then I visited a couple of classrooms. In one of the rooms, children were quietly sitting on a June day, raising their hands for a teacher to come by and check their letter L's. Sara had been writing all her letters since she was two years old. I swallowed hard and went to the next classroom. This one looked more hopeful. Children were in small groups, working on a math project. One of the boys started singing softly. "Sammy, this is no time for singing," said the teacher.

I left those classrooms and changed my mind about sending Sara to school. I talked to my husband, told him how strongly I felt, and we decided to home educate. It went completely against my background as a former public school teacher, and it felt scary but it also felt right, and we were in a position to make such a choice.

People home educate in various ways. I am somewhere to the side of *unschooling*, which means I use curricula for certain subjects like math and language. But the rest of the time my kids are doing things like washing dishes in a sled, or crashing down the hill on one, trying to miss the house.

It is not unusual for such play to result in a song. Today, in Spring, I am treated to a humorous riff on spaghetti. In Winter, the girls felt a bit more sentimental, and composed this song, as the sun was going down on their play...

Just Count the Stars

What do you do when the sky is orange
What do you do when it smells like porridge
What do you do when it's purple as a plum?
Just count the stars, one by one.

What do you do when the trees are pouring
Snow on your head and it's really quite boring
What do you do when the lamps are lit?
Just count the stars, bit by bit.

What do you do when the snow is falling
What do you do when your home is calling
What do you do when you've lost your heart?
Just count the stars, part by part.

When we are engaged in what feels like the serious business of writing, we may be reticent about regularly incorporating play into our writing habits. It might seem too childish, too outside our familiar routines, too unpredictable concerning its potential impact on our writing. Yet I have come to accept the drain-clog episodes as a kind of godsend in my writing life—a signal that I've been taking myself too seriously and need to change venues, from the writing counter to the sled.

If we don't already incorporate play into our writing schedule, we might begin by taking the drain-clog moments (the flat tire, the key that we accidentally locked in the car, the missed airplane) and using them as a chance to pull out the proverbial hose and play. If we don't want to wait for a drain clog, we can do other things like occasionally write improv poetry on Twitter (I do this with a group called @tspoetry), or participate in playful writing projects with on- or off-line friends. Or we could juggle dishes in the back yard.

Tonight, my girls finally finish the dishes, but it turns out that the friendly hose has more to offer. Now they are spraying it skyward, dancing, giggling, playing in the falling water. It is the stuff of songs.

15 Stealing Norton

Do You Work?

It starts after dinner, when I share a poem called, "One Art." I began reading poems after dinner when my husband's job changed, and he started working late, and we felt the loss of him at our table.

"The art of losing isn't hard to master," says Elizabeth Bishop's poem. The statement is so stark. Is she really serious? Can she be that immune as to continue, "so many things seem filled with the intent/to be lost that their loss is no disaster"?

The poem is a villanelle. It repeats certain lines in a set pattern. At intervals, we hear the assertion again, "The art of losing isn't hard to master." Losing. Isn't hard to master. No disaster.

Is it the promise of such poetry that tempts Sara to steal away with my new Norton Anthology, *The Making of a Poem*? What does she hear that convinces her it is worth reading about forms like sonnets, pantoums, villanelles, sestinas. These words sound intimidating to me, and like too much work to tackle.

The next day she asks, "Do you want to hear my villanelle?" I do not know what a villanelle is, though I remember once quoting Lauren Winner, who said she stopped blogging because she'd rather learn the art of something like, say, the villanelle.

"Sure." I want to hear my girl's villanelle.

Over the next few days, the conversation repeats itself in a fairly predictable pattern. "Do you want to hear my sonnet? Do you want to hear my pantoum? Do you want to hear my sestina?"

"Sure."

I am astonished by all of it, especially the sestina. Thirty-nine lines, six end-words that must repeat in a changing pattern through-out the entire poem. I take Sara's poem and compare it to what I see in the book. It really is a sestina. Not a flawless one, by any means, but a sestina nonetheless. My girl is a middle-schooler, and she is working harder than I am at the art of poetry.

When we possess a little natural talent for writing, we might be tempted to coast along. Why try to master these things called words? Isn't writing an art? Doesn't that mean we can just let things pour out as they will? I know a lot of writers who don't work very hard, thinking this is no disaster. They set down the first thing that comes to mind, and they want that to be the end of it. I have sometimes been this kind of writer, especially when it comes to poetry.

My girl is a middle-schooler. I am not. She is working hard at poetry. I am not. So I steal away and work to change the situation.

I write about Pittsburgh, and the snow melting on Penn Avenue. I write about a booted print of water, near the head of a crow (I do not know how this head came to be lost from its body, but I write of it anyway). "I wonder if this man wants water," I write of an accordian player, who is sharing a tune at the street market. There is an ocean and a ship, and a "Heinz red neon sign/drifting 'midst lost tune of accordion on Avenue/fading, fading like the light of morning over water." I work very hard. It isn't flawless, but it is a beginning.

"Do you want to hear my sestina?" I ask Sara.

"Sure," she says.

16 Monkeys & Field Grass

Do You Cultivate Your Wild Side?

A patch of dark pink wildflowers stands just beyond the little rock garden. I call them *star flowers*, though I'm sure they have a formal name. Their stems and leaves are deep green, shaped like carnation foliage. I wonder, are these wild wanderers a cousin to the flower that serves as a man's boutonnière? The patch began with a single bloom a few years ago, which I left because it reminded me of my crazy, yet oddly rich, childhood—a time when I escaped to fields that held thousands of such flowers.

Sonia likes it that I leave the patch of dark pink flowers. I mow circles around it. I also mow circles around a patch of field grass, white clover, and something that has yet to reveal itself with a bloom.

I live in a geographic area that seems to embody this motto: pristine lawnliness is next to godliness. Whole yards have never seen a dandelion. Houses are edged with juniper, azaleas, and, if they are a bit trendy, pampas grass imported from some other paradise. Violets—good for eating—are out. Buttercups—good for a simple, cheery bouquet—are out. Plantain—good for rubbing on mosquito bites—is out, out, out.

Recently, a writer friend emailed me and admitted that he accidentally typed "a monkey feels a bunny." Apparently, the monkey was supposed to be peeling a banana, but he got side-tracked by a typo. "I probably shouldn't write about that," my writer friend observed, realizing that the image was mildly disturbing, at least for those who care about purity between the species.

I answered, "This is exactly what you should write about. You don't need to end up sharing it, but you may find that you want to. Just write and describe things, without the fear of producing anything shareable."

John Gardener, author of *The Art of Fiction*, notes that when we begin describing things, even seemingly unimportant things, we find the questions we may need to be asking in our writing, as well as the possible answers. A monkey feeling a bunny is the sort of wild combination that begs for descriptive exploration, though it may take some resolve to do so. What if someone calls the godliness police? What if someone accuses us of a crazy mind?

Sonia comes in from our wild lawn and hands me a fresh-picked leaf she has harvested. "Mommy, can you rub plantain on my mosquito bite?" she asks.

I crush the leaf and rub it on the bite until there is a little circle of green water on her skin. She is satisfied that she's on her way to healing, so she goes back outside to the patch of field grass, circles it once, twice. Her hair is shining in the morning sun. Dew is shining on the pink star flowers. I suddenly remember my sister and how she loved the wild fields. My own girl, as if buoyed by my memories, takes off leaping.

17 Big Bird in China

Do You Care for Your Writing?

We are in my room. Sara is staring out the window, a bit listless today. I am working on my French. Her presence is a kind of silent question, *What do I do next?* It reminds me of Sonia's actual question a few days ago, "Mommy, what do *I* do?"

"I think you need some goals," I tell Sara. "You're older now. You can start pushing yourself more. Make a list of ten things you want to explore or accomplish."

"I won't want to do them if they're goals."

"You can think of it that way. Or you can think of it the way I think about learning French. Nobody is making me learn French, but if I don't have a goal to learn it, it won't happen. If I don't decide that I'll fill a notebook a month with French copywork, how will I progress?"

She pulls her knees up to her chest, and I go on. "Or it's like how I want to be a better writer, so I try to read a poem a day. Nobody is making me read the poems, but I know if I read them, my writing will improve."

I go back to my French and copy a poem. I don't completely understand what the words mean, but the copying helps get them into my subconscious. It helps me feel the French under my pen. The more I copy, the more words and phrases I recognize.

Sara finds a piece of paper and begins to write some goals. She writes ten. I am surprised by some like "Learn Tai Chi." Over the next month, she reads books on Tai Chi. She practices privately. She has questions I don't know how to answer, so I invite my friend Penny over.

Penny is retired, but she still has goals. One of them is to learn Tai Chi. She knows more than we do, so she agrees to come and share.

"I first heard about Tai Chi when I watched *Big Bird in China*," she says. My girls and I are sitting in the living room with Penny. Sonia sits in the green wing chair, and is smiling. Sara sits next to me, half on the maroon oriental carpet, half on the red oak floor.

"Big Bird explained that in Chinese culture everybody grows up learning that it's their responsibility to take care of their *chi*. *Chi* is kind of a way to say *energy*. One way they protect their *chi* is to practice Tai Chi. Every village has its own special kind. Everybody can do it, old people and young people." Penny pretends to be Big Bird for a minute, demonstrates a few Tai Chi moves and says it feels like swimming, just without the water.

My girls nod, watch and listen wide-eyed. They didn't know they had a *chi*. But if Big Bird has a *chi* to protect, maybe they do too. If very old Chinese people and very young Chinese people can protect their *chi*, maybe they can too. The concept of *chi* is not a part of my culture and religion. I get the idea though. We have an inner life. We need to cultivate and protect it. In my world, this is called "caring for the soul."

Writers have a kind of soul too—a creative center that can be cultivated and protected, wasted or destroyed. There are so many ways to cultivate and protect this creative center. Whole books like *The Artist's Way* will tell us how to do that, and they are worth reading.

For me, it comes down to some very simple principles...

Have goals. Goals are more powerful than habits like "write in the morning, by the window" or "write with monastery music playing in the background" or "join a writer's group that meets every Saturday after Tai Chi." Habits, as we'll discover when we are frustrated yet again because we can't seem to sustain them, are constantly in need of changing—based on whether we are old or young, with children or with an empty nest, suffering from insomnia or sleeping like a baby by 10 pm. Goals, however, will compel us to write however we can. If, for instance, we know we want to finish a chapter by the weekend, we may have to skip window-sitting for the next several days.

Rest on a weekly basis. The old idea of Sabbath isn't just an outdated religious command. It is a deeply human practice that might surprise us in its power to refresh. Foregoing our writing for a whole day will fill us up for the week to come. Try it. If it doesn't work, you can come back to contradict me.

Choose writer friends carefully. I know someone who used to share his work with a person who was jealous of his writing. This jealous person always found a way to make my friend feel like a failure. He would pick apart the writing, hold up his own as a better example, and altogether sap my friend's creative energy. Eventually, my friend stopped sharing with that person, and it was the advent of a creative confidence that led to new professional strides.

Choose share-timing wisely. When I was writing my first book and felt so excited to be engaged in an extended project, I made the strategic mistake of sharing my first chapters with a few friends, for feedback and critique. What I didn't know about myself then (but I do now!) is that early-sharing is a killer for my creativity. I paid the price on that project, ending up with a two-month bout of writer's block. I never share the actual text of a project now, until I'm almost finished with both the vision and the writing. Not every writer gets stalled by early-sharing, but it's something to consider avoiding.

Watch out for siphons. Siphons can be people who don't give us creative space. They also can be tools, technological or otherwise. Sometimes the very tools that once energized us will morph into siphons. Blogging has been that way for me at times. It is hard to release a tool when we are used to having it in our lives. It is hard to release a person, even though he or she may be hurting us creatively.

Releasing, by the way, doesn't always mean *leaving*. It can just mean setting ourselves free from the need for another person's constant approval or their unreasonable bids for our time. It could also mean finding new ways to creatively engage with a person, to turn our relationship into a source of joy and energy. The same is true for technology and other tools. Leaving might be in order, for sure, or maybe all that's needed is a quarter turn, a new series of steps.

After Penny leaves, Sara tells me that Tai Chi is like a dance. You move in rhythm to the other person, but not in a way that hurts you or them. She tells me a story about a Tai Chi master who supposedly could respond so sensitively that when a bird landed on his shoulder he could move just the right way so the bird was unable to take off. The master knew his own body, his own energy. He sensed the body and energy of the Other. He adjusted accordingly.

I say a secret prayer for my girl. I hope she will learn such a sensitive dance in life—for the care of her creativity, her *joie de vivre*, and her soul.

STRUCTURE

18 Night is Pegasus

Making Details Real and Realer

She writes a poem about the night. *Night is the moon, night is dark, night is stars.*

It is *okay.* I tell her it has a nice soft tone, good repetition. Then I venture a deeper critique, because Sonia is getting older now, and I've been listening to her poems for just about forever, and she trusts me. "Anyone could say that about the night. I wonder how you could say something that others might not say?"

I don't tell her my theories about how geography affects our writing. How I know that she, as a child of the Northeast, will see a different sky than a child near the Nile. How the air here is different from the air in Alaska, and how mourning doves settle into hemlocks in our back yard, while mynah birds nestle under stars in India. I don't compare Darwish to Goodyear, explicate on how geography led the poets automatically each to his own: *jasmine, dove, veil* versus *cactus, cattle, tree poker.*

"Make a list of night things," I advise her.

Dark, moon, stars, wolves, black, blue, shiny, night flowers, she writes.

She has separated a piece of paper into four quadrants: Spring, Summer, Winter and Fall. The only variance in her night words in each section is the addition of the word *crisp* in Fall and Winter, and the inclusion of *crickets* in Spring and Summer. Her night is much the same, regardless of the season.

"How's that?" she asks.

"Hmmm," I say. "Can you get more specific? Can you include more of the senses? What kind of night flowers? And their fragrance? Which constellations? What do the wolves sound like?"

This request for detail, more and more specific, is a request I often make of the writers I work with. My editorial team at

The High Calling laughs that I have a taboo list, which is just a list of common abstract words like: *grace, healing, sin, mercy, blessings.*

"Anybody can say he experienced grace," I tell the team. "I want to know if a writer experienced it without the writer claiming, 'It was grace.'" What I am really saying is, "I want the writer's geography—regional, familial, personal." One way to get this geography is to forbid certain abstract words and keep digging for specific ones to replace them.

Now Sonia responds to my digging. She makes a new list of words, all jumbled together. This time the list includes a few more things like a falling leaf, something scuttling, peepers and an evening primrose.

I like the evening primrose, but I am still wanting stars with names, so I ask for them.

Sonia knows the mythological figures, from listening to *Percy Jackson and the Olympians.* She knows more than I do, from all my English classes, high school and college combined. Knowing the mythological figures is part of Sonia's personal geography.

"Perseus," she says.

"That's good," I say. "Think of more specific constellations. It will give you better grist for a poem."

"Pegasus," she adds and goes away. Later she returns with a new poem…

Night is the moon, night is dark.
Night is stars, constellations.
Pegasus, Perseus, Great Bear.
Night is planets, night is rest,
night is late. Night is
prologue to tomorrow.

I could tell her that I want to know which planets: Venus, Jupiter, Mars. I could ask how she knows it is late (where's that evening primrose?). I could ask for mourning doves resting in their nests. But this poem of hers is a prologue to tomorrow's. We'll get there, maybe in a few more winters, a few more turns of Pegasus in the sky.

19 Football Cakes & Salvador

Beginning Structure

The information on Sara's page looks like streams, rivulets, little pools. She is entering the 9th grade this year and is trying to map her educational life as she has known it—a life we rarely call *school*, after all, we've been learning together through the years in a process closer to an approach called *unschooling* than its opposite, *classical schooling.*

We have read Yeats after dinner, just because. We have gone on a tea pilgrimage and learned about the Opium Wars on the way.

Birthday parties have had themes, since the time Sara was in kindergarten. We still laugh about the rock-hard Egyptian honey biscuits that were, as her grandfather said, possibly preserved through the centuries just to make their debut in our little Tudor. The girls tease me about the cake, decorated Greek-style, that somehow looked more like a football field than the Parthenon. We have worn Roman laurels, danced to Sonia's fiddle version of *Oh Susanah*. We've visited so many places with cake and candles in hand—China, Turkey, Italy.

We've also literally traveled—to France, Spain, Boston and Washington, D.C. There's been Notre Dame, open, and the Picasso Museum, closed; French baguettes eaten with strawberry-rose jam and the taste of salt-air high above the Mediterranean. Ruins of a palace moat, deep under the Louvre; Salvador Dali melting time on open plains.

And now this. This mapping. This attempt to take the evenings of poetry around our dark wood table, the cakes, the excursions to the edges of the Hudson or the Seine, and explain them to a distance-learning school, on an application that wants summaries and neat essays. Where to begin? Where to end?

As a writer, I have known the anxiety of trying to take the rich complexity of experience and put it into what Samuel Daniel called *small roomes*. Daniel said it this way in his *Defence of Ryme*…

> *Is it not most delightful to see much excellently ordered in a*
> *small roome?*

He was speaking of the sonnet. But he could just as easily have been speaking of any form of literature: the novel, the memoir, the essay.

Writers take different approaches to figuring out where to begin and where to end. A writer might find that the techniques that worked for one piece won't work for another. It is important to trust the piece itself more than any single technique for creating it. My first book's structure tumbled out in a week. And though I later had to rework and shift, the chronology is almost exactly what it was when I first set down the ideas. Then, for individual chapters I mapped; words in circles, joined by rivulets, seemed to shake free the past and help me organize my thoughts. My third book was different—a tedious process of culling from personal journals, then ordering additional research by topic, then combining all of the material in related chunks, then culling again and living with a lot of ambiguity about how it would all eventually come together.

Some of us tend in one direction more than another; I am fairly organic in my processes, rarely pre-organizing information and doing outlines. Yet this book I'm typing now benefited from a simple outline. The important thing is to have a variety of tools at hand: free writing, word-mapping, outlining, crowd-sourcing (thank you, Twitter friends, for helping me play with ideas for this book).

The other important thing is to remember that the work will ask of us what it needs. If everything seems like a big mess, at any point in the process, we can take that as a good sign. The work is trying to speak to us, trying to tell us what it needs. Our job is not to panic, but to listen and respond.

Sara is remarkably calm about her application process. We chat about her memories, about the experiences that stand out as the most powerful. One of these experiences is the Tuesday afternoons she spent for seven years, just playing with her friends in the woods (when her favorite friends stopped coming, it was hard to accept).

In the essay that says, "Write two paragraphs describing your-self," she decides she wants to use the woods to say what's essential about her. She has been circling around this emotionally-difficult topic for two years, unable to write about it in a way that satisfies her.

Will this moment, this mapping of cakes and Salvador, shake something loose and enable her to put a flood of memories into a small room?

20 Goodbye Purple Clovers

Strengthening Structure

"You should weed your garden bed," I tell Sara.

I've given up telling Sonia to weed hers, as the most she'll do is go out and inspect her little space, then come in the house and say, "Mommy, can you weed my garden?"

"You weed it," I say.

"I can't weed it. I don't know what are weeds and what are beets!"

"The beets have a reddish tinge to them," I answer, trying to get out of taking care of her responsibility. I have showed her the beets before, but she claims she can't remember and, anyway, she wonders, what if she accidentally disturbs the swiss chard?

So when Sonia is off watching an episode of *I Love Lucy*, or playing Pixie Hollow, I sometimes work in her stead. I'm committed to the idea of beets sometime by Fall.

Maybe because Sara is older, she's more open to tackling weed work. There is not much to work around, as the lettuce died—too many seeds dropped in the ground without care for spacing, so the roots weakened and the lettuce shriveled. There's still basil to hope for, and potatoes persisted though I thought I'd harvested them all before Sara prepared this ground. There is also kale. And the flame flowers deserve to flourish; she added them for a touch of whimsical beauty.

Now the garden is filled with competition. Bishop's Weed is staging its return. Grasses and purple clovers are making a takeover bid. I'm not going to weed for Sara (much), because I know she has the commitment and ability.

If a writer wants a piece to flourish, he is going to have to commit to the work of strengthening structure. Experienced writers will find they can do this themselves, with a little effort. Less-experienced writers should recognize that an editor might be able to strengthen their work, and it is not a good idea to get in the editor's way by trying to defend what the work is supposed to be saying. He would do better to watch an episode of *Lucy* while he waits, than to stand around explaining the work.

When a writer tries to explain his work to me, I will often remind him: "If you have to explain your work to a reader, that's a sign that something needs to change; remember, you aren't going to be there when the reader puts on his Land's End swim shorts and goes to the pool to relax with your words." I don't always say the part about the swim shorts, but I mean what I say: a writer's words need to stand alone, strong and clear.

There are many ways to strengthen the structure of a work:

- Search for pet words and delete them (Are you a *the* man or a *that* woman? You might be.)

- Remove repeated words within a paragraph or even in a nearby paragraph (especially distinctive ones—unless the repetition is purposeful, creating a pleasant sound or a stronger transition between paragraphs)

- Trim sentences, until they read aloud without a glitch

- Vary sentence length and complexity, to create a sense of pacing and interest

- Switch sentence order in a paragraph, to add surprise or prevent confusion

- Check for details—where's that evening primrose?

- Simplify details—purple clover is nice, until it crowds out the flame flowers

- Delete the first paragraph or the last one

• Scan down the left-hand side of a final draft and note how
each paragraph starts. (Are we prone to begin each paragraph
with the words *I* or *the* or *so*? Then we should mix it up and
not let that subtle habit dilute our writing.)

**When working on a book versus an article, we might also
want to…**

• Move chapters around to create more tension, letting
readers live with unanswered questions at first, so they'll feel
compelled to keep reading

• Delete chapters that seemed like a good idea but are no
longer supporting the direction or clarity of the work

• Include a recurring detail like, say, water or gophers.
Running images are a simple way to provide cohesion as long
as we don't overdo them

In the garden, Sara goes to simplify. She ties back her long dark
hair, takes the silver claw tool and begins uprooting. I have no
regrets when she vanquishes the Bishop's Weed. I try not to look at
the purple clovers now limp in the pile. There's the basil to cheer
me, and the kale. We might even get potatoes.

PUBLISHING

21 Lighthouse in New Jersey

Should You Publish?

"We'll be back in about ten minutes," I tell Sonia. She had wanted
to climb these lighthouse stairs. Metal-grated, dusty, dizzying.
We can see all the way down from here. We can see all the way up
from here. The top of the structure promises a view of the ocean,
right on over to New York City.

I had driven two hours South to visit a friend in New Jersey.
She'd told us about the lighthouse, oldest one in the country. My
girls wanted to go. I wanted to go. It might help us stop thinking
about Sonia's knees.

Just a week before this day, Sonia had come to me one morning and wakened me, though she knows I don't like to be wakened.

"Mommy, my knees really hurt."

I'd opened my eyes and seen without seeing. Known it was
Lyme Disease. Two months earlier, I'd picked three ticks off my
girl's sweet little body, called the doctor who said don't worry yet.
I'd watched for fever, waited for a rash. Nothing. But now in this
moment, I knew.

I sat up, pulled the sheets back. "Sonia, let me see your
knees."

Her knees were hot and swollen to three times their size.
They looked like her grandmother's knees had looked after surgery,
purply and tender. She was in pain but refused to cry.

"Honey, I'm going to call the doctor," I'd said.

Now, in the lighthouse, knees still fairly swollen, antibiotics
fighting inside her, she wants to climb one-hundred-and-one
narrow spiral steps. And I say, "Okay, you can try," because I don't
want to hold her back if she thinks it is worth the struggle. I doubt
she can make it to the top, but I don't want to make the decision
for her.

So we start, Sonia leaning into me, taking each step slowly and stiffly like an old woman. We touch stone walls, feel the coolness of the place. We lag behind the rest of the group, hear them laughing and talking above. At the halfway point, it is finally too much and Sonia can't go on. I give her a hug, look into her eyes and say, "I'll go up with Sara," because I am in a dilemma; Sara wants to go to the top, but she is nervous to go alone, and Sonia cannot move another inch. She sits down on a cold metal stair, leans against white walls. "I'll wait," she says, eyes steady, filled with longing.

Sara and I climb to the top. The last ascent isn't stairs at all, but a metal ladder with nine tiny, slippery rungs. The guide has to open a hatch so we can ascend to the lookout area. We take our turns on the ladder, and the guide closes the hatch when the last of us wriggles onto the platform.

"I can see New York City!" I say, more than once. "It's amazing!" We are taking pictures, marveling about the farmhouses to the south, the city to the north, the water to the east. We are loud, apparently, and our words slide down to Sonia, who can hear what she's missing.

After about ten minutes, the guide says, "Thanks for coming." She has told us we really need to keep to the schedule, because she has another group waiting to climb. She turns to open the hatch, to let us go back down, and I hear someone whimper.

"Mommy?"

I look down and it is Sonia.

"Can I please… come up?"

She is crying, and I catch my breath. I look to the guide and mouth, "Please?" I know the schedule is the schedule, but here is my girl with tears streaming down her face, and she has come up dizzying stairs all by herself, pulled herself past pain because she wants to see.

Sometimes writers tell me they want to write a book. I say, "Are you sure?" I don't want to hold them back, but I want them to think about what they're getting into. Two of my books plunged me into sorrow and emptiness when I wrote them. Both are memoirs, and they pull from hard places. Each was a climb I felt ready for because I'd already experienced a measure of healing. I'd told the stories in smaller pieces before—to friends, over many years.

As writers, we have to judge these things. We may not be ready. I've met writers who backed off from an idea once they realized what it was going to take. I've backed off from my own ideas I knew I wasn't ready to tackle. Sometimes the reasons can be intensely personal: we can't tell a story that is still too raw. Sometimes the reasons involve timing or a need for growth; for instance, Sara wants me to write a fiction book, and I want to do it, but I'm not ready to invest the time it would take to learn that special craft.

Sonia looks to the tour guide and waits for an answer. She looks at the last nine stairs. These are the worst; they aren't stairs at all, but rungs. No one can carry her up them. They are too narrow. They are perfectly vertical.

The guide looks at her watch. She'll be late if she extends this opportunity. But she tells my girl, "Yes."

Struggling, crying, Sonia comes.

22 Fame in the Foyer

Can You Find a Small Audience?

"Come to my cooking show," Sonia invites. I am chopping onions, my own version of a cooking show, but she won't wait. I must come now. Sit now. Watch now.

She tugs my arm, leads me to the living room, where she has placed two dark wood dining room chairs—one for me and one for her big sister. The chairs are facing our Tudor foyer, where dark trim frames a red oak staircase and sun shines through a leaded-glass window with the criss-cross diamond shapes we think of when we think of old Germany.

And might this be an old German woman's kitchen? Here is Sonia with a cornflower bandana tied onto her head like a peasant kerchief. She is wearing a red and green plaid apron over a golden and brown calico dress we made together by hand. Here is a make-shift table she has spread with a red checkered cloth that has black roosters and black-and-white cows and weathervanes. The table is cluttered with my German grandmother's worn cooking tools: a red wood-handled pastry cutter, the wire a faded grey; a red wood-handled beater; a slotted turner that's good for lifting spaetzle from boiling water. Here is a sign with large black magic-marker letters, that says, *Sonia's Cooking Show*. She's ready for the live audience and the cameras.

Before I was a writer with an audience, I was simply a friend and relative, with my cornflower bandana on my head to keep the hair out of my eyes. I wrote letters, prolifically, to my golden-haired cousin Monica, all through my childhood. When I went to college, I wrote to my German grandmother almost every week. After I graduated, church people started asking me to do short devotional talks for baby and wedding showers. Somebody asked me to do a book review for the church newsletter. Then, when I was newly-married, I was asked to speak for a church ministry on a regular basis. I did not realize that these small audiences were preparing me for a professional writing life. It is probably better that I didn't. I was free to use the casual, red-checkered cloth of my life and my thoughts, without the pressure of making something "important" happen.

It is not uncommon for writers to seek a large audience too early in their writing journeys. The idea of being published is a dream promoted by a cluttered market of writing books, writing conferences, and vanity publishers (not to be confused with print-on-demand, which is a business approach, not a kind of publisher—more on that later). I love working with new writers but am often surprised at the desire they have to pursue a publishing dream when they haven't yet put on a small-time cooking show, so to speak. (If you prefer to think in terms of home improvement shows, go ahead and substitute the metaphor. I won't mind.)

I've heard it said that most successful writers put in about fifteen years of small-audience writing before they begin to work with larger audiences. There are exceptions of course, but if every writer with a publishing dream thinks he is the exception, the math doesn't work out. Ninety-nine percent of the writer population cannot be the exception to the Fifteen Years of Writing for Your Grandmother rule.

I do not say this to be harsh or disheartening. I say this to be encouraging. If we are worried about our writing future, because at the moment we seem to be standing in the foyer with a make-shift table of old cooking tools and a magic-marker sign to announce our show, we shouldn't worry. We are exactly where we need to be. Tomorrow we might move to the front porch and entertain a few neighbors as well. This is also exactly where we need to be. The key is to keep working with small audiences, while gradually making forays into slightly larger arenas.

Right now, Sonia is in the foyer, exactly where she wants to be, with her mother and sister acting as a studio audience. I switch on my camera to capture this creative moment. I imagine that someday my girl will speak to audiences larger than this, and she might delight to look back at her German-Grandma Cooking Days.

"Welcome to Sonia's cooking show!" she says cheerily, tipping her chin up, raising the red-handled beater high in the air.

23 Linsay's Driveway

Networking

We are at Linsay's farm. I am in the stuga, and Sue, Linsay's friend, is poking through the cooler for me. She hands me sugar snap peas, lamb's quarters—which grow wild and taste like spinach—and a carton of Jemima's eggs.

"You eat duck eggs?" a curly-haired woman asks me, wrinkling her nose.

"Yes," I laugh. "I take it you don't?"

She shakes her head and wrinkles her nose again. I tell her that's fine with me, because that way we won't be competing for the eggs. After all, Jemima and Lucky each lay only one egg a day.

While I'm putting my purchase into my blue canvas bag, a white-haired man begins chuckling.

"Look at that kid. Will you look at her?"

I wonder if he's talking about one of my girls.

"Look at her all alone in the driveway, walking around with a book. It's a big book! Look at her face. She is totally into that book," he says. "Oh my God, look at her laughing. I love that."

"I bet that's my girl you're talking about," I say. Then I move to his side and look out the wood-framed window. Sure enough, there's Sara, walking around with a Sherlock Holmes pastiche. (I learned that word *pastiche* from Sara, when she explained that I was not correct in calling the book a knock-off of the original stories.)

If it were up to Sara, she would sit on the couch all day reading Sherlock Holmes, or Tolkien, or even Oliver Sacks. Sara loves books. Sara loves people too, though she is shy and sometimes will simply listen to a conversation instead of joining. She marvels at her younger sister who jumps right in, talks to anybody about anything, and will phone a friend three times in a row in span of ten minutes, without giving the friend a chance to return the call.

When we chose to home educate the children, we chose a reality that would require a little work to provide connections for our shy girl. It would also require a little work to teach our social butterfly how to enjoy solitude and give people some space.

Learning the art of both connecting and holding back are two sides of a coin we commonly call Networking. Writers need to network if they hope to get published. And they need to address both sides of the art.

I will never forget the writer's conference where Mickey (let's call him that, though I remember his real name and don't wish to embarrass him)... anyway, the conference where Mickey walked around with his clipboard, accosting anyone who looked like she might offer him a professional connection. I was sitting on a bench near a meandering stream, enjoying a morning of relative solitude, when Mickey walked up and took visual note of my Staff Badge, then asked for my name, email, and home address.

Not wanting to be rude, but not wanting to reward this behavior, I gave him my blog address and told him he should come visit me there sometime. "If we seem to develop a natural connection out of that, we could keep in touch a little more."

After the conference, Mickey visited my blog repeatedly, leaving his links every time, with requests that I go read his work. He asked for my email again, quickly invited me to connect on Facebook and on LinkedIn. I confirmed him as a friend on Facebook. I didn't accept the invitation on LinkedIn. Let's just say, we did not seem to be forming a natural connection. I felt like Mickey cared nothing about me, except what I might offer him in the world of publishing.

Not to be too hard on Mickey, the up side of what he was doing is this: He didn't suffer the illusion that he could land a publishing contract by sitting on the couch, sipping club soda, hoping he would somehow magically get noticed by editorial people who would propel him into fame as deep and wide as Arthur Conan Doyle's.

The key to networking, then, is twofold: be bold in creating connections, but do it in a way that is natural. If that sounds simple, it is. If that sounds hard, it is.

It's *simple,* because it means we can connect with anyone at any time, just by noting what we like about or have in common with a person. If we don't like a person, or seem to have little in common with him, we should pass up the connection. Nothing deep will come of it, because we won't be delighting in one another and naturally interested in promoting one another. (Yes, part of networking is thinking, "What can I offer this person, however small? Even if it's just a good chuckle while he's waiting in line at the stuga?")

It can also be *hard* to connect, because it's not like we can meet industry influencers without a little effort. Sure, it can occasionally happen serendipitously, but more often we'll need to take time and have patience, working our way from the edge of a social circle towards the center. This might sound utilitarian, but if we commit to only pursuing connections that are a good fit, there is nothing wrong with genuinely working within a system that expects us to work according to its rules.

These rules are easier to work with in certain contexts. A three-thousand-person conference will not make it simple to connect. We're not going to walk up to Marilynne Robinson after she speaks, and somehow get an invitation to eat dinner with her later that evening (ask me, I know).

A three-hundred-person conference makes things a little easier. We can take a seminar with an editor and thirty attendees, maybe ask a question along the way, and perhaps give a compliment as we're walking out the door. Maybe the compliment will make the editor happy, and she will chat with us a bit longer. Maybe that evening we could sit at her table (some conferences are organized this way), and we can see if the connection we began might deepen naturally. Or we might just end up eating our sugar snap peas, feeling a bit alone.

There are a few excellent venues that really change the odds. Laity Lodge, for instance, offers retreats that cap at about fifty attendees. Some of the seminars have limits as small as ten people. Unless we are terrifically shy, there is no reason we can't make a few good connections in such a setting.

If we don't want to go to Laity Lodge in Texas, we could try our hand at connecting online. Places like *The High Calling.org* attract some of the same writers and editors we'd find at an actual retreat. The rules for connecting are similar. Hang around with people we want to get to know. But always, always pursue connections that are a good fit and have potential to delight both parties. Find and promote the people we want to connect with on Twitter, Facebook, their blogs, the sites they write for, but again, we shouldn't expect a busy editor or influencer to take immediate note of us. Our time might be better spent making friends with people who are closer to us in the social circle, including those who are slightly more towards the center than we are.

All in all, people are very generous when they feel genuinely liked. We just shouldn't fake our networking efforts; it's not a good way to go. If we fake, we risk earning the reputation of a Mickey with his Connections Clipboard. Also, if we are genuinely trying to connect with big influencers, we need to remember they're extraordinarily busy, sometimes receiving 100+ emails a day. We shouldn't feel too sad if they don't seem to notice the beautiful duck eggs we've got waiting in the shadows of our sweet little stuga.

Today, Sara is reading Doyle, on the fringes of a social situation. She is not at home on the couch, but she is not in the stuga evangelizing either (she's a passionate believer that everyone should read Sherlock Holmes, "from the beginning, no skipping around," as she noted in one of her application essays).

When the white-haired man goes out to stand in the driveway, Sara doesn't notice him. I finish buying Jemima's eggs, the snap peas, and lamb's quarters. I go out to take a few pictures of a nun who is walking down the drive. The white-haired man watches me photographing the nun, then we begin chatting and I discover his name is Tony. Gradually, Sara becomes aware of my voice and moves closer to this social interaction I am having.

Tony waits until she is next to me, then he says, "So you like Sherlock Holmes?" She smiles, and the conversation begins.

24 Club Penguin

Would You Publish You?

"Josiah told me about this cool game called Club Penguin," Sonia says. "Can I try it?"

I ask her to bring up the site. I'll take a look at it and make a decision. The site is less attractive than Pixie Hollow, another virtual world she got a subscription to on her birthday. Club Penguin also appears less complex and possibly less educational, but the penguins seem safe enough. I know that Sonia mostly wants to be able to say she has played the game, dodged the super-snowballs; it's a social thing, a conversation she wants to join. So I acquiesce.

She starts the registration process, and I leave the room, but before I can get down the stairs, she is already yelling to me, "Mommy, I need a credit card!"

A credit card?

Turns out Club Penguin has a $5.95 monthly cost. But I have already said yes, and though I prefer not to pay the $6.00 (it's really six dollars, I tell her), I keep my word. Yes, she can play Club Penguin. Here's the credit card, for the first and last time regarding this particular club. "If you want to extend the membership after a month, you'll have to pay for it yourself," I tell her. I already know we'll be giving her another year of Pixie Hollow, and I prefer not to pay for this additional game.

The month passes quickly. Penguins slide in the snow, maybe sip a few dripping icicles, maybe go Polar-bearing. When I realize the subscription is about to auto-renew, I ask Sonia what she wants to do. She goes away to think about it and comes back with $6.00 from her hard-earned Tooth-Fairy Cash Stash. *She would like the nickel in change.* I see she is getting the hang of this money thing.

Another month goes by, and the penguins are still having snowball fights. She's been hit in the eye a few times and attacked by a group of unfriendly penguins. But there are still accolades to achieve in the world of Winter. Will she dig into her Pooh bank again, for the privilege of staying in the game?

Every so often, a writer who has had no luck in the game of getting a contract will ask me about having his book published, maybe with a Press where I have connections. In response, I usually have one of two conversations with the writer. One, I might encourage him to consider self-publishing, using a print-on-demand business approach. Or, two, I might offer some advice, which is really not advice at all, so much as it is two questions...

Would you dig into your cash stash, for the privilege of playing the publishing game? Would you publish you?

People sometimes think that print-on-demand is a cheap alternative for an author who publishes on his own. It's a business approach, and it's less expensive than traditional publishing, since books are only printed when they are ordered by a customer. There is no need for warehousing and inventory systems. Artwork is uploaded simply and quickly. Distribution can be obtained through traditional channels like Ingram. It really is a terrific approach both for authors who have a platform and for small presses. (I've also heard tell of some traditional publishers reviving out-of-print titles by switching them over to print-on-demand.)

Regardless of who is publishing print-on-demand, to do an impressive job there are costs involved—art and design, editorial, publicity, to name a few. For good quality services, the costs can run into the thousands. This is one reason traditional publishers are so careful about granting contracts (reputation is another); their initial costs can often be as high as $10,000 (the exception being if they're reviving an old title, which has already been through the editorial and design process).

Small presses using print-on-demand must make the same careful decisions. Will the profit from sales outweigh the initial costs? Will the author be a good addition reputation-wise? Will the author promote titles other than his own, understanding that an author who does this is often promoting the health of the Press, ultimately benefitting his own book? These considerations can give perspective to a would-be author. Maybe he can understand now why he couldn't get a contract.

If, however, the would-be author believes he could sell a lot of books, because his website is wildly popular and he is regularly speaking or being published at major magazines or online venues, then he should be happy that the traditional publisher accidentally passed by his work. With self-publishing royalties that can amount to earning $6 to $7 per book sold, this is significantly more than he would have earned per book with a traditional publisher. He can also buy his book at cost, sometimes as low as $2 to $3, and make an even tidier profit when he sells it at a speaking engagement.

It is not a perfect system, as it usually prohibits book returns. It can also be less advantageous to go-it-alone than to work with a Press whose titles buoy each other in the marketplace. Still, self-publishing using print-on-demand is a solid alternative for the author who has perfected his craft, built his platform, and isn't intimidated by the prospect of finding vendors to supply excellent editorial and design services.

"I'm going upstairs to play Club Penguin," says Sonia. This is the last day she'll be choosing this alternative, she tells me, as she won't be paying to renew.

"Are you sure?" I ask. "You won't be able to talk to Josiah about the penguins anymore."

She assures me she's fine about letting her Club Penguin membership expire. She's happier at Pixie Hollow, where the fairies are beautiful and they don't cost her a nickel.

25 Basil & Beets

Delusions of Grandeur

"Maybe I can sell my vegetables at a sidewalk stand," says Sonia.

I smile inwardly, remembering my own childhood, and summers at my grandmother's house. My sister and I would rise early, go out into the moisture-thick morning, and pick tomatoes or cucumbers, yellow squash or corn. Sometimes we'd go to the weeping cherry and lose track of our mission to fill little baskets with sweet fruit. I imagine it was my grandmother who did the real harvesting, who made it possible for us to set up a roadside stand and sit for hours in the shade of the giant mulberry trees, waiting for a customer.

Most of those roadside memories are a blur. I can't remember any actual sales, though I'm sure we made some. I do remember that a couple once stopped and paid us five dollars to take our picture. I guess they wanted to artistically capture two brown-haired girls, probably in cotton dresses made by our grandmother, probably stained purple with the cherries or the mulberries.

Now my own girl is dreaming the same kind of agricultural sales dream. There is no mulberry tree to offer shade. There are no fields teeming with fruits and vegetables. There's just a concrete sidewalk, narrow and summer-hot. There are two garden beds in a back yard, struggling to grow beets and basil. What can she realistically hope for? I'm not sure.

During the early, hopeful stages of writing this book, I started a Twitter chat one morning. I asked my writer friends what they would like to see in a book on writing. Bradley J. Moore said I should talk about delusions of grandeur ("not that I've had any," he joked). I laughed. I know all about delusions of grandeur. I've had my share, even though I knew the following information before getting my first book published...

According to a Chris Anderson article in *Publishers Weekly:*

- *950,000 titles out of 1.2 million tracked by Nielsen Bookscan sold fewer than 99 copies*

- *another 200,000 sold fewer than 1,000 copies*

- *only 25,000 sold more than 5,000 copies*

- *the average book in America sells about 500 copies*

- *fewer than 500 sold more than 100,000*

- *only 10 books sold more than a million copies*

Somewhere in that list is my first book, and it isn't in the last bullet point. Or even the second-to-the-last bullet point. It isn't in the first two either, which was a small gift. However, because I am mildly protective about my identity, I didn't even get my picture taken. (Good thing, because I'm usually wearing a cotton T-shirt, and it's not uncommon for it to be a little stained with berries or tomato sauce.) So much for delusions of grandeur.

Personal delusions aside for a moment, these book-sales statistics surprise me, from the standpoint that any publisher would offer anybody a contract, knowing the probabilities for financial "failure." In the current economic climate, and the rapidly-changing publishing game, it seems to be more and more of a gamble to publish anyone at all. Grandeur as *delusion* is likelier than ever, not just for authors but also for traditional publishers.

Still, there is a market. We shouldn't give up our dreams altogether. We just need to consider how to reach it without eating all the profits along the way. Keeping production costs to a minimum (print-on-demand sounds better and better!), choosing a solid content-focus that matches our target audience, and seeking as many free publicity avenues as we can are all part of the mix. It is no secret that much of this can be done in an online context, and it is worth watching those who do it successfully, like Darren Rowse, Seth Godin, and FastCompany.

Now I open the back door, make my way to inspect the girls' gardens. Sara's basil is growing fast and beginning to bolt. I nip the lavender flowers to keep it from going to seed, to assure that the leaves will stay strong and large.

Between patches of wild sorrel and unidentified bright green weeds, Sonia's garden has three small beets growing. They are about four inches tall, a bit spindly, but we have a few months to see if they'll ultimately thrive.

I'm guessing there won't be a sidewalk stand, unless we want to share our three beet bounty with a kindly neighbor who decides to buy from two brown-haired girls. But we may yet stain our own fingers, by laying the beets across the cutting board, and making a few fine cuts.

26 Cactus on the Way

Don't Go Alone

It is still daylight, and we love the sea. We have come to forget, to touch the water, to smell the salt air. So far, we've climbed the stairs of an old lighthouse and it is still hours until sunset. We haven't put our toes into sand, found shells, braced ourselves together against the waves and laughed.

But Sonia is tired.

We get in the car, make our way back off this peninsula. The water is calling. "What do you think?" I ask. "Do you still want to go to the beach? I'm not sure Sonia can really do this." Both girls want to go.

I find a turnoff to the ocean, park as close as I can. It is September, so the beach is all but deserted. I park in a handicapped spot, because there are so many, and no one is here except a lady walking her dog.

Camera in hand, I walk slowly with Sonia. Sara goes on ahead. She wants the waves, and they are far, far out. I take pictures of cactus (I didn't know cactus grew in New Jersey), a caterpillar in the sand, pink flowers.

As writers, we sometimes choose to pursue a particular work, or the hard path to publishing, even though the odds seem against us. We're drawn by a vision—it is the water, or the cactus in unexpected places, or the pink flowers.

Yet as we continue moving we realize: someone is going to be too offended by what we write, or we may not be able to stay resilient under the pressure of schedules and the need to balance commitments, or the journey is long and uncertain. Sometimes we get where we are trying to go writing-wise and discover the world doesn't care if we falter, as long as we keep serving up the kind of words they've come to expect from us. Sometimes we don't get anywhere near where we thought we'd go, selling far fewer articles or books than we ever envisioned, and we feel we've failed.

When these things happen, do we have someone to carry us? Have we developed a smaller community who really cares about us as people, about our creativity and our essential selves? A community that is not going to judge us too harshly, or be too jealous of our successes, or lack compassion when we don't "succeed"? These are questions worth asking before we need their answers.

"I can't walk anymore," says Sonia. Her knees are hurting. By now, Sara is out of sight, having turned the corner beyond a large beach building that blocks our view of the ocean. I cannot take Sonia back to the car without telling Sara. And, anyway, Sonia still wants to see the water. So I put my camera in my bag and lift my girl. She puts her head against my chest, goes limp in my arms.

I question my sanity. Why in the world am I here with my girls, when one is so tired and in pain?

"We came to forget," I tell myself. "We came because we might as well be in the presence of beauty while this Lyme disease is trying to take away my girl's strength. We came because a bed wouldn't change anything, except to make my girl sad and focused on her illness."

I walk on, hold Sonia close, look down and put my face in her brown hair. I can hear the water beyond the turn.

GLITCHES

27 That's Not What Happened

Writing the Truth

We finish cleaning up watercolors, brushes, books on Chinese art. We put away tea-box templates, old tea catalogs, and business plans the kids have made for their imaginary tea establishments.

For seven years, almost every Tuesday, my girls have been coming to this room with their home school friends. The first few years, I stayed downstairs and participated in the bible study with other parents. About five or six times a year, I spoke from the podium, learning as much about writing and speaking as I was learning about Ephesians or Romans or Isaiah.

When the Audobon specialist I hired couldn't work with the home school group anymore, I shifted my focus and came upstairs. I've been teaching Hebrew or Spanish and art for several years now. I look forward to discussing how the greatest Titanic artist in the world, for instance, started from a place of initial rejection (his work was too realistic, they said). I've shared my discoveries of how someone like Georgia O'Keefe always saw through eyes of *place*, even painting her cityscapes in a way that somehow mirrored the striations of the canyons that had early-impressed themselves on her mind. The kids and I have sung about chickens in Spanish, "Pio, pio, pio!" We've traveled to worlds of French Art Nouveau, Russian ballet, folk Appalachia.

After our explorations, it's always been the same. The kids go off to play in the woods or they hide in the art closet sharing secrets. I sit on this floor with my grown-up friends and chat about education techniques, struggles to balance commitments, the joys and challenges of working with our kids, or maybe the latest books we're reading that are keeping us fascinated with life beyond our borders.

More and more, though, this too has shifted. One day we showed up to find the art closet locked. New policy, we learned.

The kids were puzzled and disappointed. One day we showed up to find "Posted" signs all along the ridge to the woods that leads to what the children call The Great Ravine. The kids were angry, "How could they? Who did this? Our forts! Can we at least go in and get the pieces of blue and white pottery?" The woods now closed to them, they started playing in the nooks and crannies of this log-cabin church, with its meandering design. Two years ago, some of Sara's favorite friends stopped attending the program. With those kids gone, and the woods now all but closed, Sara has, more and more often, preferred to sit here with the grown-ups, as she is today.

"You inspired me," I say to my friend Anne. "I started writing my book." She smiles, strawberry-blonde hair playing across her shoulders.

"I'm calling it *Rumors of Water*," I say. "I love that the title came from Sara's words at the picnic. I wrote about that in the first chapter."

Sara and Anne both lean forward to protest, "That's not what happened!"

"What do you mean?" I ask.

"I said there was ice but there weren't any cups," Sara asserts.

"It was me who said there were rumors of water," Anne says.

"You have to change your chapter," says Sara, eyes steady, face set.

Most of what I write is memoir-based. I weave together ice cubes from picnics past, crayfish from the creek of my childhood, halting journeys up old lighthouse stairs. I have a mind for details, so I'm able to recapture what it felt like to be somewhere, both physically and emotionally. Still, there are occasional protests, "That's not what happened."

Others in my life remember things differently. They may be correct in saying that the apron was not blue-striped at all, but red and green plaid. Though both aprons are in my life, I misapplied the scene where the blue one shows up. If someone tells me before I publish, I might change the detail. I want to share the truth, after all.

This question of details and truth has arisen with the editorial team I help manage online. "Can this really be true?" an editor asks. "Can the writer really remember to this level of detail? Should we run the article like this?"

Sometimes the editor has a strong reason to question: another party has already protested behind the scenes, about a serious detail, "That's not what happened."

I ask the editors to think about it this way: Has the writer been as true as she could be? Has she captured the main gist of the experience, even if a peripheral apron might have been red-plaid instead of blue-striped? If an actual protest has been made about some aspect of a story, I ask, "Is the rest of the story true, to the best of our knowledge? Whose truth are we relying on? Does the center of the story seem to be supported by several reliable parties? Can we consider removing the questionable part and run the rest of the article?"

Often, I can tell when a writer has engaged in a little embellishment. Everything fits together too perfectly. Details seem tailor-made for the philosophical point of the story. The villain gets caught at exactly the right moment. I suspect a bit of creative tinkering, yet I know this is a hunch I can't prove. After all, once a writer begins to look for patterns, he's almost sure to find them in what happened, and a good writer will bring these patterns to the surface with cohering details.

How accurate are the details? Maybe it doesn't matter, if a detail is peripheral. Maybe it does, if that peripheral detail is going to make or break someone's reputation. How much can a writer alter the details, by accident or on purpose, before he's changed a rumor into an unacceptable reality?

"I'm not changing it," I say to Anne and Sara. "It's my first chapter!"

They shake their heads, wide-eyed. They are witnessing what they believe to be a trespass. I have attributed rumors of water to my daughter instead of my friend, and now I want to keep it that way, for the sake of creative coherence.

"It's okay," I say. "It's perfect, really. I'll add a chapter later in the book, on the sticky problem of truth in our writing. I'll reveal that it wasn't Sara who made the rumors comment. I'll tell about the ice cubes and the cups. I'll let my readers know the gist of the story was true, even though I mixed up a detail."

They lean back, and I can almost hear their breathing slow—at least in my writer's imagination.

28 Pixie Hollow

Alternating Realities

"I want to play with my pets, or they'll go away," she says. It's been more than a week since Sonia has visited her virtual home in Pixie Hollow, so I say yes, go play with your pets.

She goes to her home in the hollow, where she takes on the identity of a fairy she named Pearl Mistystream. She bought Pearl a *water-talent house*, which Sonia claims is messy. I laugh. "Not too different from real life, huh?" She laughs in reply.

The house, located on West Elm Creek, is filled with blue-frosted cupcakes, 35 bottles of dye (including sour plum), a pumpkin coach with clocks for wheels, tables and sea-shell staircases with pin-and-thread banisters, ice sculptures and purple feather curtains. A hummingbird flits around the room, happy to see Sonia's fairy, maybe waiting to be fed blueberries. "You have to feed them berries or they leave," she explains to me.

I don't want her to lose her hummingbird, but I say, "You can play for just fifteen minutes today. We're going to go for a ride on the bike trail in a little while."

Sonia protests. It is hard to leave one world for another.

We writers know all about that. Whether playing with ideas or trying to finish just one more chapter before we have to feed somebody, or feed ourselves, it can be hard to put away our pen and switch realities. If we refuse to make the switch, we may find ourselves in a variety of less-than-optimal situations. Ideas begin to come more slowly, because we've forgotten to take time with a real seashell or a real creek. We've let our bodies get frozen into position, and our brains are not as likely to fire with creativity or solidify learning. Sometimes we get cranky. Maybe the hummingbirds in our lives feel like flying away.

It is important to take the time to move body and soul. Walking, biking, dancing, pillow fighting, whatever. Brain scientist

John Medina notes that physical movement and engagement of multiple senses jumpstarts thinking. Similarly, it has long been known that physical touch affects mood; babies who suffer lack of touch in orphanages die early and old people who get a pet to cuddle die late.

On the bike trail, I hang back with Sonia. At one point we stop to rest on a wooden bench. She reads the dedication inscription and I note that the birth date is near my mother's. The death date is September 11, 2001. I pull my girl a little closer before we get back on our bikes.

We pass swamps filled with soft pink roses that smell like bubblegum. We pick black raspberries and wine berries, and we get in a conversation about my grandmother's cherry trees. A tiny blue butterfly flits past, and I share that I used to chase this kind of winged creature in my grandmother's fields. Sonia begins singing happily, "Oh my darlin', oh my darlin', oh my darlin' Clementine..." I take note of the way the wind feels on my skin and consider that tall green rushes may have taken their name from the way they sound: *rushes-rushes-rushes-rushes*. We stop at Dragonfly Pond. This is the place where powder-blue dragonflies hover and dart, and fish float like tiny brown sticks in jade algae-jewel-encrusted water. A tiny tree in the center looks as if it's bearing miniature apples. I silently muse that this place seems like a fairyland.

"I wish I could take a dragonfly home for a pet," says Sonia. "Daddy wouldn't be allergic. What would I feed it though?"

Today, back in my writing world, I think of Sonia's wish for a dragonfly, and I ask her to tell me more about her Pixie Hollow pet. I learn that her hummingbird's name is Lightningcliff and that he's a boy. I learn that she can make him happy by playing a game with him. It's a flying game, where the fairy flies under the bird. If the hummingbird begins to fall, the fairy uses a pillow to bounce it back up.

"Ligtningcliff is almost full-grown," she tells me. "That's when I'll have to let him go." It's just a hummingbird in a make-believe world, but I turn away and cry.

29 Hula Hoops & Red Balloons

Rejection

"Nobody liked my idea," she says, her voice wavering.

We are driving past the farm with the big white house, where they put red balloons out near the mailboxes, to invite us to stop and purchase yellow squash or cucumbers, pickled onions and relishes. Since making it a weekly habit to go to Linsay's farm, we haven't made an effort to turn into this other drive. Not since last year, when we fussed with trying to dig out the proper amount of cash to put in the lock box and gathered a few tomatoes into a paper bag, wishing we knew whose hands had picked the red goodness and placed it at the mouth of this farmland.

The balloons are waving in the breeze, as if to say, "Pick me, pick me." I feel a slight desire to answer with a turn of my steering wheel, "Okay, here we are." But I drive on. And, in any case, Sonia is in tears.

"Nobody wants to do the circus this year. Some of the kids said it was a dumb idea," she cries a little harder now, for the addition of insult to loss.

It is *loss,* because this is a tradition she and her friends started about four years ago. At the end of the year, in the big room with the art closet, they have entertained the younger children who have also been meeting in a separate group all year. The younger kids have climbed stairs to find hula hoopers and The Lovely Laughing Lady, human pyramids and cello players, songs by girls in matching red plaid dresses and popcorn-filled paper bags painted circus style. This is one of Sonia's favorite parts of the year—a chance to use her passion for comedy and staging, a chance to make the children happy, a chance to do something fun with her home school friends.

In the writing life, rejection is common, for a variety of reasons. All of it has a chance to teach us something. Much of it is good news, in an odd way. If, for instance, we have offered our

writing to a publication, and we have done so before polishing
our craft, it is a benefit to our reputation that our piece be rejected,
so we don't end up with inferior work attached to our name.
Of course, the publication isn't thinking of our professional
advancement when they reject the piece. They are concerned about
their reputation in the eyes of their particular audience.

Audience matters, and is another consideration we need
to keep in mind. But sometimes we're so concerned about getting
published in a certain place that we offer up a mismatch. The publication sees it right away. The voice doesn't fit, or the kind of
topic. They might get hundreds, even thousands of misfits, and
they will give a resolute *no* that can feel heartless to the writer.
It is up to the writer to learn from such mistakes, to ask himself,
did I pitch this in the right direction? For instance, for a long time I
tried to get published in journalistic-style magazines. Then one day
I realized I really don't like journalistic writing; the publications had
known this longer than I had, since they'd said *no* to a lot of my
misfits. It was a good day when I caught up to their *no*'s and
realized I would say *no* to me too, for that particular kind of
writing; clearly, my work was better suited for a different editorial
stage.

Often, if a piece is a good match, it can still be rejected
because of editorial needs. The publication just ran a piece on
gophers and residential SWAT teams last month; they don't need
mine on the gopher-ousting success of gasoline and matches.
Closely related to this are the needs of the editors to work with
writers who make their jobs easier or more pleasant. If we are
always showing our teeth and carrying spears, and the next writer,
just as talented, is sharing his bag of popcorn and making an
editor's day, it should be no surprise that we might need to adjust
our approach.

Regarding book contracts, the reasons for rejection are
similar. Style, overall fit, the set of existing books (they don't need
another *DaVinci Code*; they already have one), our temperament,
our platform. Again, these editors might receive hundreds, even
thousands of proposals. They can't take the time to say a lengthy

and compassionate *no*. If they do, this is often a terrific compliment; we should consider it a kind of affirmation about the work, or us, or our platform.

I try to affirm little Sonia now. "Oh, Honey, it's a good idea. Some of the new kids don't know what it's like to do that kind of show. They don't have the same good memories and the motivation. And the time is so short, too. You'd only have a week to put it together."

"But…" she is still crying, refusing to be consoled.

"I'm so sorry, Sweetheart," I say gently. "Maybe you can do it next year?"

No, she will not put it off until next year. She will ask Lydia to help her. Lydia is one of her best friends and they will make it happen together. She is quite sure. She will email Lydia as soon as she gets home.

It is not going to work out, this year or next, but neither of us knows that today, driving past these red balloons, towards the river that runs to the sea.

TIME

Experience Takes Time

It is raining, and I don't feel like going to Linsay's farm. I chide myself for telling her just last week, "You've hooked me. I love coming. I'll be here every Friday."

Reluctantly, I gather the girls, make the trip, even though I suspect that the rain will probably mean no table set with an apple-printed cloth, no glass pitcher with mint and lemon water, no raw honey for drizzling. We pull into the long gravel driveway. The horses are not in the fields, nor by the fences. They prefer the warm dryness of their stables. "I can't pet the horses today," laments Sonia. We walk past the empty corrals to the stuga, past old-fashioned white roses, and pink. I decide not to photograph the roses—not in this rain.

At least we will see Linsay, I think, looking forward to her easy smile, her strong yet delicate way of moving, her small-talk about strawberries or the high nutritional content of Jemima's eggs or how she is recovering from the incident with her runaway dogs (they took her across the gravel, and her shins show the evidence).

I peek into the quiet stuga. It is shadowy this stormy day, since it depends on natural light. The rain has made it damp, and I can smell the old wood. Kale and swan-like garlic stems fill a wicker basket. I smile at the woman who is flipping through the little notebook on the counter.

"Linsay here today?" I ask.

"She has a wedding this weekend. Went out of town."

"Oh," I say.

I poke around in the wicker baskets, decide against the strawberries, which I think are too moist and sure to be soft. "Got eggs today?" I ask.

It turns out that Linsay is the one who gathers Jemima's eggs, so there aren't any for sale. I am disappointed that I don't seem to be collecting what I wanted from this day.

Sometimes as writers, we want to gather everything into a single place. We can't fathom the idea that it is okay for something to go missing in an article, a poem, or a book. I struggle with this myself—fretting over the picking-and-choosing that any good work requires. I have wanted to tell all my stories in one book, as if a single book could really hold all my stories. I have wanted to make all my points in one article, as if my thoughts on a subject could really be contained in one article.

Maybe we are like the voice in a poem by the 17th-Century Indian poet Tukaram, saying, "I am looking for a poem that says Everything/so I don't have to write/anymore." Maybe we have a hard time thinking that a reader might come back to us, for more stories later on. Or we want to prove ourselves to be very clever or comprehensive. So we stuff too much into a piece of writing, instead of narrowing our choices.

I leave the stuga with a narrow cardboard box—loosely holding collard, lettuce greens scattered with nasturtium, and sugar snap peas. Last time I forgot the sugar snaps, because I got so carried away talking to Linsay. This time I purposely leave the strawberries.

Back in the car, we are now wet from the rain. Sonia asks where the strawberries are and I have to apologize. I hadn't realized she'd wanted them. I'm sorry I missed buying them, and I can't go back, because I pay by check and I only had one check with me.

On the way out, I slow down, until the sound of tires crunching gravel stops. I hadn't noticed the little graveyard before, but there it is under tall cedar trees. I fumble my camera out of the black bag, roll down the window, and take a few pictures of old stones. My girls are talking at the same time, "Is it a family graveyard? Is it very old? The stones are kind of plain." I listen to their voices, and the thought crosses my mind that every time I come to this farm I find something I missed before.

31 Watering the White Moth

Writing Takes Time

As I water her garden, I think of my dark-haired girl—Sara, who weeded and planted and worked this ground. I think of the spray from the hose, how it sometimes stirs a white moth from the grass. The moth might rise into the arc of the temporary rainbow made by my watering. But there is no moth today.

At fourteen, Sara is no longer the child I used to put to bed with a story, though she still loves Narnia with its dwarves and lion, its thick woods, endless sea and elusive white stag. She is now a writer in her own right, who chases the past and tries to stir it up from the grass of memory, in a way that pleases her as much as the arc of a rainbow.

I love this about her. That she somehow agrees to circle back and stir, knowing she still has more to say about a particular memory. That, even though the memories sometimes hurt, she is willing to return to them, to do the work of creatively weaving them into a thing of beauty.

For a few years now, she has been trying to write about the woods where she used to play with her friends. In a piece I included in another book, she had written, "No matter how hard I try, I can't seem to write about the woods."

This year, when completing her application for the distance-learning school, she once again tried to stir her memories. "Write two paragraphs about yourself," the instructions said. She wrote more, because two paragraphs couldn't contain the self she wanted to present, the self standing at the edge of the woods looking back, not sure she could yet look forward...

> *She is standing on the edge of the ravine.*
> *It is cold out; the trees and the forest are the brown of* winter.

*She has played here every Tuesday for years, with all the
others: There are the Meeting Rocks, black in the afternoon light,
where all important decisions were made, and the sapling in front
they once clutched as they jumped to the ground.*

*There are the ropes strung across the ravine, a zip-line
that never worked, and a handrail along a fallen tree.*

*There is the fallen tree that was once a bridge, and the
bridge next to it of boards and rocks and branches.*

*There is the New Fort, a hidden place, with a swing and
a rusty grill, and a cookie-tin full of broken pottery in glazes of
many colors.*

*There is the Sculpture Tree with green glass bottles and
cans strung from its branches, full of water from the rain, and the
seesaw tree in the muddy center of the ravine.*

It is cold.

*She is standing on the edge of the ravine, standing on
fallen leaves and remembering the winter they made a sled to run
down the almost-vertical path onto the ice. It was the top of a
sandbox and black plastic bags.*

It is silent.

*Silent, and strange, now that everyone is gone. Lonely,
and frightening, and wild.*

Memories fill the woods like crocuses in snow.

I believe a writer can *make* writing happen, sit down and stir from
grass or leaves or snow. But I also believe it takes *time* to write.
Each book I've written, in some sense, could not have been written
before its time. The white moths were not ready to rise.

Part of what makes them ready is the commitment to come
to the edge of our memories and keep bringing them upward.
This can take many years. At the start, the commitment might feel
like nothing at all. It might take the shape of complaints offered in
secret to friends. It might take the shape of anger or tears. It will
almost always become stories, released in dreams or in our waking
hours. We might tell others these stories, each time adding a new

detail, or we might scribble our memories into the small rooms of poems and private journals.

There is no hurry. The things we cannot write about today, we will surely find we can write about tomorrow. We should not worry about the process, but simply trust it and move on. After all, we contain fields upon fields of stories we've rehearsed over time. We must recognize that these are the ready ones, the now-stories.

When I stand at the edge of the garden, I water with a certain kind of faith—that the water I am spraying now will make Sara's basil grow, that this rainbow in my hands is beautiful and is enough for today, that somewhere between clovers and strawberries is a white moth that may yet rise.

Living with Time

Sonia circles the room carrying a white wire basket on her head. "It's a medieval laundry basket," she tells me.

We have come here late today, just as the service was getting out, right before the coffee hour that is held in this big room— the same room where my girls have been meeting with their home school group for what amounts to most of their lives. Both of my girls have also grown up in this church. They know its winding hallways, its hiding places and closets, the brown metal side door that sticks in summer and slams in winter.

On the way upstairs to this room, I hugged the girls' grandma. "Good to see you here today," I said.

She smiled and leaned on her cane. It's her first time out since the knee surgery, many weeks ago. "Good to be here," she said and walked towards the front entrance.

The front entrance has never felt like a front entrance. Nobody uses it that way, as the parking lot is near the side door. Today the side door is dark, plywood covering its window. People got the idea that we should renovate and turn the side door area into a big entrance. We are going to get an elevator for congregants like Grandma, so they don't have to leave during coffee hour, frustrated that they can't climb the stairs and join in the social time.

Today we drink tea upstairs, chat with people who are sipping coffee and eating bagels. We chat until the last person leaves us in this big room with its tan paneling and beige berber carpet. Sonia now circles with her medieval laundry basket, each time moving closer to the gaping hole of the renovation. The stairs we have used every Tuesday for years are gone. The art closet is gone, the only evidence of its existence being some jagged wood edges and all these art supplies stacked near the piano.

I look at the gaping hole, covered in plastic, and it reminds me of a nightmare I had when I was little. There were stairs with a black hole at the top. A wild wind blew, and my mom was sucked up the steps. I screamed but no sound came out. I grasped for her feet, her clothes, anything to keep her from leaving me. The wind was too strong.

Now my Sara, who has refused to look at the renovation hole, and the plastic weeping inward, sits at the piano. She opens the cover, and it feels like a statement. "I am here." She is facing the hole without glancing at it. I recognize the first song as *Andante*, by Johann Christian Bach. It moves slowly, like a sad dream, and my throat tightens.

Sonia circles past me and accidentally drops her wire basket on my arm. "Sonia!" I say too loudly. She is playing, but the basket hurt. "I'm sorry," I say. "I know you didn't mean to drop it. Here's your laundry basket." I hand it to her, and she inspects its invisible stash before putting it on her head and skipping off again.

What makes this Office Max® basket *medieval?* From the looks of its vinyl-coated wire, I'm not sure, but Imagination sees beyond *what is* to *what can be.* I smile inwardly, to think that my girl jostles invisible apples and maybe a black-bird pie, as she attends a feast of her own making.

Sara's piano music has changed to *Pomp and Circumstance.* Images of me as a young woman, in a high school white cap and gown, flood my mind. I remember the cut of my hair, *feathered* as they used to say. It wasn't the best style for my face. The memory gets mixed up with images of Sara, sitting here at the piano, playing a tune I suspect she doesn't know has anything to do with graduation.

I pull out a piece of paper and begin scribbling words. I want to remember this music, this moment. Now Sonia is digging through the art supplies in the corner, pulling out various items like white pine blocks and a large berry-colored bottle.

The music changes again. *Joyful, Joyful, We Adore Thee.* The first hymn I ever taught the girls. We used to sit on the couch and sing together, memorize the words…

Melt the clouds of sin and sadness;
Drive the dark of doubt away…

I relate to the sadness. I am conscious that the music and the medieval laundry basket and my scribbled words are some kind of prayer, perhaps, or a form of liturgy rising from the very stuff of our lives, to creatively meet this moment.

There is more to the moment than just this room with its gaping hole. I learned the other day that the home school group is ending. Each family finally found it necessary to move on. There will be no more Spanish songs, no more watercolors, no final circus performed for little ones kicking the metal legs on their chairs.

Now Sara is improvising. And it contains everything. Wild notes pressed hard, chasing each other up the keyboard. Notes in strict rhythm, like a military song. Notes whispering and notes crying and notes dreaming, until the final note ends soft.

Sonia is pouring me an imaginary drink from the berry colored bottle, her small hands moving delicately. I hold my imaginary goblet, join the feast.

"What are you pouring for me? Water?"

She turns the bottle upright, looks to the ceiling, then back to me. "Probably wine," she says.

When did she stop pouring water, I wonder. When did it turn to wine?

"Cheers," I say. And raise my glass to my girl.

End Notes

Chapter 2

page 17   "When Our Women Go Crazy": Julia Kasdorf, *Sleeping Preacher* (Pittsburgh, PA: University of Pittsburgh Press, 1992), p. 7.

Chapter 3

page 22   "I suddenly remember Natalie Goldberg's": Natalie Goldberg, *Writing Down the Bones: Freeing the Writer Within* (Boston, MA: Shambhala, 2010).

Chapter 4

page 25   "thinking of Anne Overstreet's poem 'This Has Been a Summer of Moths'": Anne M. Doe Overstreet, *Delicate Machinery Suspended: Poems* (Ossining, NY: T. S. Poetry Press, 2011), p. 42.

Chapter 8

page 41   "You should read *Second Nature*": Michael Pollan, *Second Nature: A Gardener's Education* (New York: Grove Press, 2003).

page 41   "an excerpt of his book": Michael Pollan, *The Omnivore's Dilemma: A Natural History of Four Meals* (New York: Penguin, 2007).

page 42   "a book like *The Artist's Way*": Julia Cameron, *The Artist's Way: A Spiritual Path to Higher Creativity* (New York: Jeremy P. Tarcher/Putnam, 2002).

Chapter 9

page 47   "chance to read *The Art of the Sonnet*": Stephen Burt and David Mikics, *The Art of the Sonnet* (Cambridge, MA: Belknap Press of Harvard University Press, 2010).

page 48   "for the Ann Voskamp stage": Ann Voskamp, of HolyExperience.com <http://www.aholyexperience.com>.

Chapter 11

page 55   "A book comes up: *Tea With Jane Austen*": Kim Wilson, *Tea With Jane Austen* (London: Frances Lincoln, 2011).

Chapter 13

page 64   "from reading *Clarice Bean*": Lauren Child, *Clarice Bean: The Utterly Complete Collection* (Somerville, MA: Candlewick, 2008).

Chapter 15

page 73   "I share a poem called 'One Art'": Elizabeth Bishop, *Elizabeth Bishop: The Complete Poems 1927-1979* (New York: Farrar, Straus, Giroux, 1984.

page 73   "with my new Norton Anthology": Mark Strand and Eavan Boland, *The Making of a Poem: A Norton Anthology of Poetic Forms* (New York: W. W. Norton & Company, 2001).

Chapter 16

page 78   "John Gardener, author of *The Art of Fiction: Notes on Craft for Young Writers*": John Gardener, *The Art of Fiction: Notes on Craft for Young Writers* (New York: Vintage Books, a Division of Random House, Inc., 1991).

Chapter 17

page 82   "when I watched *Big Bird in China*": Children's Television Workshop (now Sesame Workshop), *Big Bird in China* (New York: NBC, May 29, 1983).

Chapter 18

page 90   "from listening to *Percy Jackson and the Olympians*": Rick Riordan, *Percy Jackson and the Olympians Boxed Set* (New York: Hyperion Book, 2008).

Chapter 19

page 94   "Samuel Daniel called 'small roomes'": Sameul Daniel, *Defence of Ryme*, in Stephen Burt and David Mikics, *The Art of the Sonnet* (Cambridge, MA: Belknap Press of Harvard University Press, 2010).

Chapter 25

page 122   "According to a Chris Anderson article in *Publishers Weekly*": Chris
Anderson, "A Bookselling Tail," *Publishers Weekly* (July 14, 2006)
<http://www.publishersweekly.com/pw/by-topic/columns-and-
blogs/soapbox/article/6153-a-bookselling-tail-.html>.

Chapter 28

page 138   "John Medina notes that physical movement": John Medina, *Brain
Rules: 12 Principles for Surviving and Thriving at Work, Home, and School*
(Seattle, WA: Pear Press, 2008), p. 17, p. 207-208.

page 138   "babies in orphanages die": Ben E. Benjamin, Ph.D., "The Primacy
of Human Touch," at BenBenjamin.net <http://www.benbenjamin.
net/pdfs/Issue2.pdf>.

page 138   "old people who get a pet to cuddle,": author uknown, "Older People
and Companion Animals," in *Private Client Adviser* (Volume 9, Issue 4,
June, 14, 2004). <http://www.ecadviser.com/xq/asp/
sid.0/articleid.20594568-56F2-4BB7-814F-47731141CBD5/
eTitle.Older_people_and_companion_animals/qx/display.htm>.

Chapter 29

page 142   "they don't need another *DaVinci Code*": Dan Brown, *The Da Vinci
Code* (New York: Anchor, 2009).

Chapter 30

page 148   "17th-Century Indian poet Tukaram, saying, 'I am looking for a
poem'": Tukaram in Daniel Ladinsky, *Love Poems from God: Twelve
Sacred Voices from the East and West* (New York: Penguin, 2002),
p. 340.

Chapter 31

page 151   "Lewis and Narnia, with its dwarves and lion": C. S. Lewis, *The Lion,
the Witch, and the Wardrobe* (New York: Harper Collins, 1994).

Chapter 32

page 156   "music has changed to *Pomp and Circumstance*": Sir Edward Elgar, *Pomp and Circumstance No. 1.*, (1901).

page 157   "Melt the clouds of sin and sadness; Drive the dark of doubt away": Henry Van Dyke, *Joyful, Joyful, We Adore Thee,* poem set to Beethoven's *Ode to Joy* in Symphony No. 9.

Also from T. S. Poetry Press

Barbies at Communion: and Other Poems,
by **Marcus Goodyear** (Best Poetry Book 2010 Runner Up,
Englewood Review of Books)

Marcus Goodyear's poems are portable, easily carried in the mind,
tightly compressed and deceptively simple, like a capacious tent
folded into a package you can tuck in your backpack.

— John Wilson, Editor, *Books & Culture*

From Barbies to tea bags and credit cards, from broken pipes
to communion wafers and mowing dead grass, Marcus Goodyear
moves us through our world. His juxtapositions of the convention-
ally sacred and profane reveal to us the falseness of our conven-
tions. Where the vision is large, all is sacred.

— John Leax, author *Tabloid News*

God in the Yard: Spiritual Practice for the Rest of Us,
by **L.L. Barkat**

Mix Richard Foster and Annie Dillard in a blender, and you'll pour
out *God in the Yard...*

— Ginger Kolbaba, editor Christianity Today's *Kyria*

L.L. Barkat's wise words move us more deeply into matters of
consequence.

— David Naugle, author *Reordered Love, Reordered Lives: Learning the
Deep Meaning of Happiness*

All T. S. Poetry Press titles are available online in e-book and print editions. Print editions also available through Ingram.

Follow T. S. Poetry Press on Facebook at http://www.facebook.com/pages/T-S-Poetry-Press/149822048417893

If you blog about *Rumors of Water*, please feel free to **share your post link on our T. S. Poetry Press Facebook Wall.** We'd love to hear your thoughts.

CPSIA information can be obtained at www.ICGtesting.com
Printed in the USA
LVOW072142291211

261686LV00002B/17/P